The Role of Departmental Secretaries

Personal reflections on the breadth of responsibilities today

The Role of Departmental Secretaries

Personal reflections on the breadth of responsibilities today

Andrew Podger

THE AUSTRALIAN NATIONAL UNIVERSITY

E PRESS

Published by ANU E Press
The Australian National University
Canberra ACT 0200, Australia
Email: anuepress@anu.edu.au
This title is also available online at: http://epress.anu.edu.au/dep_secs_citation.html

National Library of Australia
Cataloguing-in-Publication entry

Author:	Podger, A. S. (Andrew Stuart)
Title:	The role of departmental secretaries : personal reflections on the breadth of responsibilities today / Andrew Podger.
ISBN:	9781921536816 (pbk.) 9781921536809 (pdf)
Series:	ANZSOG series.
Subjects:	Government executives--Australia. Australia--Officials and employees.
Dewey Number:	352.3

Cover design by John Butcher

Funding for this monograph series has been provided by the Australia and New Zealand School of Government Research Program.

John Wanna, *Series Editor*

Professor John Wanna is the Sir John Bunting Chair of Public Administration at the Research School of Social Sciences at The Australian National University. He is the director of research for the Australian and New Zealand School of Government (ANZSOG). He is also a joint appointment with the Department of Politics and Public Policy at Griffith University and a principal researcher with two research centres: the Governance and Public Policy Research Centre and the nationally-funded Key Centre in Ethics, Law, Justice and Governance at Griffith University. Professor Wanna has produced around 20 books including two national text books on policy and public management. He has produced a number of research-based studies on budgeting and financial management including: *Budgetary Management and Control* (1990); *Managing Public Expenditure* (2000), *From Accounting to Accountability* (2001); *Controlling Public Expenditure* (2003); *Yes Premier* (2005); *Westminster Legacies: Democracy and Responsible Government in Asia and the Pacific* (2005); *Westminster Compared* (forthcoming) and most recently *The Reality of Budget Reform in the OECD* (forthcoming). He is completing, with John Butcher and Ben Freyens, a study of service delivery in the Australian government, entitled *Policy in Action* (with UNSW Press). He was a chief investigator in a major Australian Research Council funded study of the Future of Governance in Australia (1999-2001) involving Griffith and the ANU. His research interests include Australian and comparative politics, public expenditure and budgeting, and government-business relations. He also writes on Australian politics in newspapers such as *The Australian*, the *Courier-Mail* and *The Canberra Times* and has been a regular state political commentator on ABC radio and TV.

Table of Contents

Foreword

It is a rare privilege to read a personal career history in which so many of the principal features allow for reflection and others are instructive of later developments in the role of departmental secretaries in our system of government.

I have observed Andrew Podger's career in the Australian Public Service since the 1970s with interest, admiration and gratitude for the insight and competence he has assiduously given to his increasing responsibilities.

It is timely that the history of reform in public administration over three decades is recorded in this monograph and revealing to study relationships with Parliament and government. It is important that leadership development of public administrators should be a leading objective.

Andrew's understanding of the support valuable to a minister invokes personal recollections and experience. My first ministerial appointment was in the Fraser Caretaker Government in 1975. The support of the secretary and the officers of the Department of Education is remembered with respect. The Prime Minister's guidance to new ministers was to value and seek the advice of the department. This was indeed pertinent advice, not only initially but throughout my ministerial appointments from 1975 to 1983.

I noted Andrew's comments about differing approaches from ministers with regard to Section 64 of the *Constitution*. I must say that I was always conscious of the appointment 'and to administer the Department of' and I found that the closest collaboration with the departments of Social Security and Finance resulted in the effective implementation of government policy. All ministers are bound by cabinet's authority and they should ensure that cabinet is fully informed of the political and whole-of-government outcomes of decisions taken.

Andrew was exemplary in his anticipation of information needed to support a cabinet submission or to defeat a conflicting Expenditure Review Committee imposition. The close association with my office was enhanced by the inclusion of a staff member from the department to facilitate a valuable forthright exchange of views and information.

This monograph is remarkable for the breadth of experience it discloses through changes of government and some of the questions posed are signposts to the future. I am confident that Andrew will continue to be a contributor to excellence in public administration as it adapts to the needs of modern and sound government in Australia.

Margaret Guilfoyle
March 2009

Dame Margaret Guilfoyle was Minister for Education (1975), Minister for Social Security (1975–80) and Minister for Finance (1980–83). (Photo by kind permission of the Parliamentary Library.)

Preface

The purpose of this monograph is to provide a comprehensive description of the role of a departmental secretary today, how that role has changed, the range of issues involved in exercising that role and some lessons from my experience.

Some of my predecessors have written on aspects of the role (for example, Crawford 1954, 1970; Cooley 1974) or provided a formal enunciation of the role (for example, Codd 1990). There is also some previous academic commentary such as Spann (1976, to the Coombs Royal Commission) and Weller (2001). This account, however, is both more comprehensive and more contemplative, drawing illustrations of the full range of work involved and the challenges faced from my personal experience. It is also, of course, more contemporary. Appendices A and B to the monograph summarise my career in the Australian Public Service from 1968 until 2005, including the departments I headed between 1993 and 2002, my time as Public Service Commissioner from 2002 to 2004 and the ministers I served.

It is written primarily for those who might be secretaries in the future and for those working closely with secretaries including ministers and ministerial staff as well as other senior public servants, with summaries of the lessons I learned that others might find helpful. In addition, I hope it is informative for a wider readership of officials at all levels and parliamentarians, academics, students of government and others who work closely with the political process such as journalists, lobbyists and senior people in business and non-governmental organisations.

The responsibilities of secretaries are substantial and even those who interact frequently with them rarely see the full picture. From time to time, some elements will hit the headlines, sometimes as a success but more often as a failure or a scandal when responsibility is quickly sheeted home to the minister and the secretary. The wider context (including whether either the minister or the secretary was or should have been involved) and the full range of work being done are, however, rarely appreciated. Political and media judgments of performance often rest on narrow perspectives, which may or may not accurately reflect overall performance.

Government has also become more complex and ministers and senior public servants are facing greater challenges than in the past. There might be more players on the stage of national politics and public administration, and the Public Service has long lost its pre-eminent position, but this has not diminished the role and responsibilities of secretaries: indeed, it has generally added to them.

Notwithstanding the changes to the Public Service during my career, there is also much that remains substantially the same. The basic principles and values under our Westminster traditions have remained relevant. The notion of a career public service attracting and retaining some of the best and the brightest with lifetime commitment to the Australian community is still important, despite the benefits and reality of increased mobility; and wider participation in the political process has not overshadowed the important role of the Public Service. Being a departmental secretary is a particular privilege, with wonderful opportunities to influence public policy and to inspire and support public servants whose job it is to ensure the delivery of quality services to the public.

I am grateful for advice I received from a number of people, most importantly John Wanna, Pat Weller, John Nethercote, David Stanton and Helen Williams; I also received helpful comments on a late draft from the two ministers with whom I worked most closely, Brian Howe and Michael Wooldridge. My wife, Barbara, provided much more than moral support, commenting on drafts, reminding me of relevant incidents and assisting with word processing and layout.

Andrew Podger
March 2009

Photo: Andrew Podger when Secretary of the Department of Health and Aged Care (photo by kind permission of the Department of Health and Ageing).

1. Responsibilities of secretaries

The formal responsibilities of departmental secretaries are set out in the *Public Service Act 1999* in Section 57:

(1) The Secretary of a Department, under the Agency Minister, is responsible for managing the Department and must advise the Agency Minister in matters relating to the Department.

(2) The Secretary of a Department must assist the Agency Minister to fulfil the Agency Minister's accountability obligations to the Parliament to provide factual information, as required by the Parliament, in relation to the operation and administration of the Department.

The *Public Service Act* also requires agency heads to promote (not just uphold) the Australian Public Service (APS) Values and binds them to the Code of Conduct (ss 12, 14).

The *Financial Management and Accountability Act 1997* also identifies special responsibilities for what it terms 'Chief Executives' (Part 7). These include in particular (s. 44) that they must manage the affairs of the agency in a way that promotes the proper use (that is, efficient, effective and ethical use) of Commonwealth resources for which the chief executive is responsible.

These two acts, and the regulations and directions made under them, establish the generic framework within which all departmental secretaries operate: their responsibilities, their authority and their accountability. Employees of their departments must obey their lawful directions and secretaries may issue Chief Executive Instructions. They must present annual financial statements to the Auditor-General that give a true and fair view of the finances of the department and they must provide an annual report to their minister for presentation to the Parliament in line with the requirements of the Joint Committee on Public Accounts and Audit.

Each secretary also has specific responsibilities. The Administrative Arrangements Order issued from time to time by the Governor-General on the advice of the Prime Minister sets out for each ministry the areas of responsibility and the legislation to be administered 'by the minister'. In the case of the Health portfolio, nearly 50 pieces of legislation were listed in 2001 (and more now). Most but not all are administered by the department and, in many cases, there are specific references to the powers and responsibilities of the secretary, or of the minister who in turn delegates them to the secretary.

Table 1.1 Health and ageing legislative responsibilities

The Administrative Arrangements Order in 2001, when I was the secretary, set out the functions of the Health and Ageing portfolio and the legislation administered by the minister. Among the 48 pieces of legislation listed, the following provide a flavour of the responsibilities involved:

Aged Care Act 1997

Australian Hearing Services Act 1991

Gene Technology Act 2000

Health Insurance Act 1973

Home and Community Care Act 1985

National Health Act 1953

Quarantine Act 1908 (relating to human quarantine)

Therapeutic Goods Act 1989

Most of these acts authorise the secretary and/or the minister (who frequently delegates authority to the secretary) to make decisions exercising public power over individuals and organisations in order to deliver services, provide benefits or regulate behaviour, and hold them responsible for how that power is exercised.

For example, under the *Aged Care Act 1997*, the secretary is responsible for approving aged-care providers (s. 8) and planning and allocating places (ss 12, 14). The secretary mostly delegates such powers to officers in the department, but is held responsible overall for the management of the program and the exercise of the delegated powers. I was made acutely aware of this on several occasions, as mentioned in a number of later chapters in this monograph (see, for example, the 'Kerosene baths' case in Chapter 3).

In addition, in exercising their generic and specific responsibilities, secretaries are bound by administrative law and, in some cases, may hold specific authority under the legislation.

Table 1.2 Examples of administrative law provisions

Under the *Administrative Appeals Tribunal Act 1975* (s. 25[4]), the tribunal has power to review any decisions under any act. Secretaries or their delegates are constantly making decisions under various laws, which are therefore subject to possible Administrative Appeals Tribunal (AAT) review.

Under the *Administrative Decisions (Judicial Review) Act 1977* (s. 5[1]), a person aggrieved by a decision may apply for an order of review on a wide range of grounds, including a breach of natural justice, that legal procedures have not been observed and that the making of the decision is an improper exercise of power.

Under the *Ombudsman Act 1976* (s. 5[1]), the Ombudsman shall investigate administrative action by a department where there is a complaint, and may on his own motion investigate any administrative action, with reports going to the minister and, if he is not satisfied with the department's response, to the Prime Minister and possibly the Parliament.

Under the *Freedom of Information Act 1982* (s. 9[2]), 'principal officers' (including secretaries) are responsible for making documents available and making arrangements for decisions; under s. 36(3), ministers are responsible for any certificates denying access to internal working documents on public interest grounds—a power frequently delegated to secretaries.

Legally, the responsibilities of secretaries relate to the operation and administration of the department and the programs the department manages. In practice, the responsibilities go much wider. Since the late-1980s, the term 'portfolio secretary' has come into common use. It does not appear in legislation. It reflects, however, the expectation that a secretary will help the minister to coordinate the activities of the multitude of agencies reporting to that minister (Table 1.3). This is particularly relevant in a portfolio with several ministers, one of whom has overarching responsibilities and sits in cabinet, and where there are quite a few agencies, big and small, in addition to the department. The 'portfolio secretary', for example, is responsible for helping the senior minister to prepare the 'portfolio budget submission' and will ensure preparation of the 'portfolio budget paper' for Parliament, and will probably be present throughout Senate Committee hearings on budget matters, including those relating to the agencies over which the secretary has no legal authority.

***

Table 1.3 Health and ageing: portfolio agencies in 2001

- Aged Care Standards and Accreditation Agency Ltd
- General Practice Education and Training
- Australian Institute of Health and Welfare
- Australian Radiation Protection and Nuclear Safety Agency
- Food Safety Australia New Zealand
- Health Insurance Commission
- Health Services Australia
- Hearing Services
- Medibank Private
- National Blood Authority
- National Health and Medical Research Council
- National Institute of Clinical Studies Ltd
- Private Health Insurance Administration Council
- Private Health Insurance Ombudsman
- Professional Services Review

In addition, there is a large number of independent committees, councils and authorities (many statutory) without their own employees—for example, Pharmaceutical Benefits Advisory Committee, Medical Benefits Advisory Committee, Australian Community Pharmacy Authority, Gene Technology Standing Committee, Pharmaceutical Benefits Pricing Authority.

***

Aspects of this portfolio responsibility have more recently been formalised after the Howard Government's response to the *Uhrig Report* on the governance of statutory authorities and statutory office-holders. This provides a role for secretaries in advising on appointments and on performance, while not constraining the statutory responsibilities of the authorities and office-holders involved. The Rudd Government has since strengthened the role of secretaries (and the Public Service Commissioner) further in providing advice to support merit-based selection of agency heads and statutory office-holders.

Secretaries also have a collective responsibility, partly reflected in the Management Advisory Committee (MAC) (*Public Service Act*, s. 64) to which all secretaries must belong. Significantly, the fact that the Prime Minister appoints secretaries (s. 58) makes it clear that, notwithstanding their formal accountability to their own ministers, they are to serve the government as a whole.

Introduction of performance-based pay for secretaries in 1999, although since dropped, provided an opportunity to summarise the different dimensions of the responsibilities of secretaries for the purpose of assessing their performance. The then Public Service Commissioner suggested five criteria—support for the minister, support for the government as a whole, management, leadership and promoting the APS Values—to which subsequently was added a sixth: implementation of government decisions. The APS Commission's Senior Executive Service (SES) leadership capabilities also provide a useful insight into the skills required at the top of the Public Service to perform competently. These are summarised under the headings 'shapes strategic thinking', 'communicates with influence', 'cultivates productive working relationships', 'achieves results' and 'exemplifies personal drive and integrity'.

These responsibilities are in fact very broad, so the first questions I address (in Chapter 2) are how much time secretaries spend on the range of responsibilities with which they have been charged and what personal styles different secretaries use in meeting their responsibilities.

The remainder of this monograph is structured around the following headings, which encompass the range of responsibilities and the main areas of personal activity from my own experience:

- Chapter 3: Support for the minister
- Chapter 4: Support for the Prime Minister, cabinet and whole-of-government processes
- Chapter 5: Working with the Parliament
- Chapter 6: Management of the department
- Chapter 7: Management of the portfolio
- Chapter 8: External relationships (including with other governments and with non-governmental organisations and businesses)
- Chapter 9: Working with the media
- Chapter 10: Promoting the values and contributing to APS capability.

Chapter 11 addresses the development of and personal support for secretaries, and performance appraisal. Chapter 12 examines the role of the Public Service Commissioner, which differs in important ways from that of secretaries, with its own issues and challenges. Chapter 13 sets out some final comments and conclusions.

2. Know and pace yourself: personal style and time allocation

The time secretaries devote personally to different aspects of their responsibilities depends on a number of factors including the functional responsibilities and size of the portfolio and department, the style of the minister(s) and the personal preferences and style of the secretary.

Personal style

Personal style is not a minor factor. Notwithstanding the development by the APS Commission of its generic SES leadership capabilities, each secretary (and each SES officer) has his or her own style of leadership. This affects how they do their job as secretary and how they allocate their scarce time. Being aware of this themselves is also important, to be mindful of the importance of roles that are not natural strengths but require personal effort and also to look to others in the senior team to complement their own strengths and preferences.

Among the secretaries of my era (first as an SES officer and then as a secretary of three successive departments) who I admired and learned from, there was a significant variation in styles:

Tony Ayers (former Secretary of the departments of Defence, Aboriginal Affairs, Social Security and Health and Community Services) was a wonderful manager of people and had a keen sense of what was feasible: a can-do operator rather than a policy analyst, close to ministers, with a great political 'nose', a delegator of authority to others (but insisting on being kept fully informed)

Ian Castles (former Secretary of the Department of Finance and Australian Government Statistician) was the top intellectual throughout my time in the APS, a careful researcher and analyst and consummate presenter of the evidence at the right time, but allowing others to lead in the management of his agencies

Mike Keating (former Secretary of the departments of the Prime Minister and Cabinet, Finance and Employment and Industrial Relations) was a driver of reform, a hands-on developer of policy with government ministers and a hard task master demanding prompt implementation

Helen Williams (former Public Service Commissioner and secretary of many departments, including Education, Tourism, Immigration and Multicultural Affairs, Information Technology and the Arts, and Human Services) was always insistent on rigour, whether in advice or in financial management, putting great effort into marshalling the expertise and resources of her agency while always taking personal responsibility for the advice given and the programs managed.

All of these devoted considerable time to supporting their ministers, but while Ayers would be in frequent personal contact by phone or in meetings, Williams divided that with marshalling the work in her department and testing it for accuracy and appropriateness; Castles would be doing personal research and analysis with a small number of key staff; and Keating would be personally switching between ministers, his own officers, officers in other agencies and senior people in the states to drive the reforms he was enthusiastically pursuing, looking for common ground without compromising anything he regarded as important.

Table 2.1 The Castles' policy art

Ian Castles' personal contribution to policy research and advice was extraordinary. His staff tended either to love him for this or to despair, as he appeared to ignore other matters. I was clearly in the first camp, perhaps because I was fortunate to find our interests often coincided.

I had the privilege to work with him on family allowances reform (1976), income tax reform (1977–78 and 1985) and superannuation reform (1983 and 1985), among many major policy initiatives. He had a great sense of timing and a brilliant capacity to identify a radical alternative option and to present the arguments in favour—he was never happier than when taking on well-entrenched views, either within the bureaucracy or among famous outside commentators.

An example of his style was his paper 'Economists and anti-economists', prepared for ANZAAS in 1984 when he was Secretary of the Department of Finance.

This paper, much larger than an article but shorter than a book, was ostensibly about the role and contribution of economists in the century after the publication of *The Wealth of Nations* in 1776. It was also, however, a comprehensive rebuttal of internationally prominent scholars and television presenters Kenneth Clark and John Kenneth Galbraith who had been misrepresenting economists to pursue their own agendas, and a cry for economists to continue to contribute to the scientific study of social and economic issues. Castles marshalled the resources of the National Library of Australia to help him demonstrate the concern for public welfare of economists such as Adam Smith, Thomas Malthus and David Ricardo, and their challenging of the establishment of their day, taking on power and privilege gained from abuse of markets and from inadequate government involvement in areas such as education, and promoting what were radical views at the time on matters such as civil liberties and the role of women.

Castles spent hours for days at a time in the National Library preparing this superb paper, managing, for example, to draw on personal correspondence during the Irish potato famine. The paper, however, had no direct impact on current policy, let alone on financial management.

Did he neglect his other duties? There were those in the Finance department who felt he did, but I look back on the 1980s as the period during which Finance built its reputation as a powerhouse of policy and financial management reform. Castles' efforts inspired many to raise their standards of policy analysis, emphasising research and evidence.

Peter Walsh (Minister for Finance, 1984–90) has since written that, despite rarely seeing Castles, he was impressed with the quality of written advice Castles provided and the support provided by the whole department under Castles' leadership. He said that, when they did meet, Castles spoke to him as if he were at a university seminar.

I suspect that in allocating time to different responsibilities, Williams put more effort into managing her department than the others, ensuring its financial robustness in particular. Ayers also gave particular emphasis to management matters, in his case focusing very strongly on people. Whichever department he led, he also played a major role in mentoring people and advising heads of the Department of the Prime Minister and Cabinet (PM&C) on succession management. Keating and Castles spent more of their own personal energy in developing and advising on policy, Castles being probably least involved of the four in managing the department, relying extensively on other senior officials to help him in that role.

There have also been some secretaries I have not admired. Their styles also varied, but the aspects that I most disliked were the effort of some to win personal political favour at the expense of rigorous policy advice or proper process, and the willingness of some to avoid responsibility or to bully and attach blame to others, including within their own organisations, in order to curry favour.

Allocation of time

Summarising my own allocation of time in different departments is not easy. I have no data on the time I spent at home on various activities and only limited records of time in the office or attending external meetings. It is also not always easy to allocate particular activities to one of the range of responsibilities listed in Chapter 1. Moreover, some activities are cyclical, such as the budget and Senate Committee hearings, requiring some way of averaging time allocation over the year.

The following is a very rough estimate of my allocation of time as Secretary of the Department of Housing and Regional Development in 1995, as Secretary of the Department of Health and Family Services in 1997 and as Secretary of the Department of Health and Aged Care in 2000. On average, I would probably spend between 50 and 60 hours each working week in the office or elsewhere on departmental business and another 10 to 15 hours a week working from home. This pace was maintained for the 11 years I was a secretary or Public Service Commissioner, though a similar effort was also required when I was a deputy in the Department of Defence and a division head in the Department of Finance.

Table 2.2 Time allocation

Area of activity	Housing and Regional Development 1995 (%)	Health and Family Services 1997 (%)	Health and Aged Care 2000 (%)
(a) Supporting the minister	50	35	40
(b) Supporting the government as a whole	<5	<5	5
(c) Working with the Parliament	<5	<5	<5
(d) Management of the department/agency	15	30	25
(e) Management of the portfolio	<5	5	10
(f) External relationships			
—with other Commonwealth agencies	5	5	<5
—with other governments	10	10	10
—with non-governmental bodies	<5	10	5
(g) Contributing to APS capability	<5	<5	<5

A number of activities could be allocated to several of these areas. A key rule in preparing this table is that I have allocated time involved in policy analysis or review to 'supporting the minister' where my work was on specific policy matters leading to advice to the minister; if it involved broader management of policy advising, including policy forums in the department, I have allocated it to 'management of the department/agency'.

The Health department is a large organisation, in a large portfolio with extensive stakeholders and interest groups. Despite the huge policy agenda involved, it is not surprising that I spent more time on management and on external relationships there than I did when in the Department of Housing and Regional Development, which has a far smaller policy-oriented department. I had more time when in the Housing department to contribute personally to the policy agenda and to APS capability matters (this was the period when the *Public Service Act* was first being reviewed).

The increased time with the Parliament in 2000 reflected a period of intense scrutiny of the health portfolio and my decision to lead the departmental team personally during the relevant Senate Committee hearings.

I suspect my personal interest and capacity in policy contributed to the allocation of time to policy development throughout my time as secretary, and similarly I might have spent more time than some colleagues on external relationships, particularly beyond the confines of government (for example, with academics and international networks).

Changes over time

As discussed in more detail in later chapters, there has been a shift in the balance of responsibilities particularly as a result of the public sector reforms during the 1980s and 1990s. These increased the management responsibilities of secretaries, both in running their departments and overseeing their portfolios, and tended to reduce the time they could personally devote to policy development and review.

The expectation of greater responsiveness to ministers, and of helping them manage the pressures they face from the 24/7 media cycle, has also made it more difficult to devote personal time and departmental resources to longer-term policy research and analysis.

Nonetheless, heads of Commonwealth departments are still expected to contribute more personally to policy development than those heading state departments.

The pressures of the past 20 years might also have caused some convergence of styles and possibly some increased emphasis on generalist skills among secretaries. This has been offset in part, however, by greater mobility in and out of the Public Service, including at more senior levels. The mobility is still modest and most external appointments are of people well experienced in the public sector, albeit more nowadays have state government backgrounds. While there has been movement from the top level of the Public Service to academia, the private sector and the community sector, there has been little if any real movement in the other direction.

Any convergence of styles has also been offset by modest improvements in gender diversity. Williams is no longer the only female departmental secretary, particularly since the appointment of three women in 2004 along with Lynelle Briggs as Public Service Commissioner. I well remember the coasters Sue Vardon (CEO of Centrelink, 1997–2004) gave me for my office in the APS Commission calling for 'five in five' (five female departmental secretaries within the next five years); she was one of many pleased to see the shift occur so quickly. That shift will almost certainly continue, as female representation in the APS is steadily moving up the hierarchy.

Issues concerning styles and competencies

The increase in management responsibilities has reduced the time secretaries have to focus on high-quality policy advising. This impact can be exaggerated, however. Commonwealth departmental secretaries still spend considerable time personally on policy advice and on marshalling policy analysis in their departments. I believe the overall quality has diminished for the reasons outlined above, but many secretaries still have formidable competence in their various policy fields and can and do win the policy arguments against the views of external 'experts' in confidential ministerial forums. Notwithstanding the emphasis on generalist skills (which are indeed important, particularly those relating to deep understanding of parliamentary and government processes), most secretaries do have considerable expertise relevant to the particular responsibilities of their departments.

The increase in engagement outside the Public Service has also given senior public servants wider perspectives than they might have had in the past, from which to draw on when giving advice. Moreover, arguably, the increased involvement of external groups in the political process has offset some of the reduced capacity within the Public Service.

A perennial criticism of the senior echelons of the APS has been that they represent a narrow and privileged group in the Australian community with a common orthodoxy about social and economic policy. I do not share that view, notwithstanding the obvious fact that white, Anglo-Saxon males have dominated the SES since Federation, and the many efforts (my own included) to ensure better opportunities for women and Indigenous people in particular to succeed in the APS.

As Ian Castles highlighted some years ago, the APS is not a bastion of privilege and it might be that the senior echelons are more representative of their society and culture than counterparts in other countries. The APS certainly does have further to go, but it leads most state public services (though not some overseas, such as New Zealand and Canada) and private sector companies in the employment of senior women and Indigenous Australians. With the exception of people with a disability, the trend lines for senior jobs are consistently in the right direction in terms of broadening participation. Mobility is also increasing, though modestly.

Table 2.3 Secretaries: an elite class or a reflection of an egalitarian, upwardly mobile community?

Ian Castles defended the Public Service against criticism in the 1980s that it represented an elite and powerful class. He did so by detailing the personal background of the then five most recent Secretaries to the Treasury, highlighting how many came from modest family backgrounds and had risen to the top through great personal sacrifice along with strong family and government support.

The four secretaries I have highlighted as people I particularly respected and learned from over my career also have varied backgrounds.

- Tony Ayers was born in modest circumstances in Fitzroy. The son of a junior public servant in the Customs Service, he had a good education through scholarships including to St Kevin's College. He also supported his education for a while earning pocket money working for an SP bookie. He gained a social work degree and then worked in Victorian prisons as a parole officer before joining the Commonwealth.
- Ian Castles was from Sale in country Victoria, where his father was a hardware merchant. He completed his schooling at Wesley College after attending state schools in Sale, going on to do a commerce degree at Melbourne University.
- Mike Keating was also brought up in rural Victoria, by his widowed mother, who relied on her War Widows Pension while he was young. He gained various government scholarships to pursue his education, going on to complete an economics degree at Melbourne University, and later obtaining his PhD.
- Helen Williams was born in Adelaide but spent much of her childhood in England, where her father was a senior academic in economics. She completed a history and sociology degree at Reading

University, a 'redbrick' establishment. She returned to Australia when her father was appointed Vice-Chancellor of Sydney University.

None of the four could be said to have come from a highly privileged background. Two progressed from modest rural backgrounds and one from the inner Melbourne working class.

My own background is middle class. My father was an engineer in the NSW Public Service and my mother a casual teacher at Asquith Girls High School. I am one of seven children and attended public schools in Sydney until my final two years at Shore before going to Sydney University, completing a science degree in pure mathematics.

The criticism of a narrow orthodoxy among secretaries is harder to refute, partly because the nature of the job virtually precludes secretaries from holding extreme views. Most do have strong personal views of broad policies that would enhance the public interest, while also accepting absolutely the right of the elected government to set policy. Most, and certainly the best, are not blinkered in their views but are genuinely open-minded and are keen to find the relevant research and analysis, including evaluation of past policies. There are nonetheless some common threads about the benefits of free trade and well-functioning markets, with governments intervening only where clearly justified in order to redistribute resources to those not able to rely on markets, to address market failures and to provide public goods and to support social capital. All those whose views I know believe firmly in a very substantial role for government to enhance the wellbeing of Australians. Beyond these broad threads, however, there are wide variations of views among secretaries: from liberal to conservative, from strong support for redistribution to strong belief in self-reliance, from philistines to disciples of the arts, from mathematicians and physicists to historians and sociologists to economists and accountants.

A related criticism even harder to refute is the 'clubbish' nature of the departmental secretary clique in Canberra. I have certainly found great support through regular informal lunches with colleagues. It is lonely at the top and such networking provides valuable opportunities to compare notes. For years, I shared the common criticism in the 1970s of the Commonwealth Club as the centre of public service power, yet for a long time failed to see that our lunches were not really all that different.

Table 2.4 Tony Ayers' club

In the 1970s, it was de rigueur for permanent secretaries to be members of the Commonwealth Club. A challenge for some Whitlamite appointments was to break down the barriers to this perceived establishment power base including by widening membership. I recall vividly the evening Marie Coleman, Chair of the Social Welfare Commission, was escorted to the club for dinner by Sir Frederick Wheeler, Secretary to the Treasury.

By the time my generation joined the ranks of secretaries, most of us shunned any association with that apparent bastion of establishment power. Tony Ayers had already set the example with his working-class club, the Emperor's Court Chinese Restaurant in Yarralumla. We joined him there or met at other no more salubrious restaurants around Canberra.

My pride in our rejection of prestigious places of establishment power was effectively pricked, however, when a member of my staff told me bluntly: 'Wherever you blokes meet is the centre of establishment power in Canberra.'

People appointed from outside do face a challenge if they are not included quickly into such networks. Stephen Duckett (Secretary of the Health department, 1994–96) certainly told me how much he appreciated our invitation to him to join the lunches Tony Blunn (then Secretary of the Social Security department) and I hosted of heads of the social policy departments at that time, finding these enormously helpful for breaking into the Canberra scene.

I am not sure that the reliance on such informal networks is unique to the Australian Public Service. All governments have elaborate systems for collective decision making and anyone wanting to influence decisions has to build formal and informal networks; it comes with the territory. Perhaps, however, the networks in Canberra can present an obstacle to the broadening of perspectives that might be expected from an increasingly mobile public sector executive workforce.

Lessons about time and pace

Secretaries generally work very long hours, in the office and at home. Most spend at least half a day every weekend just trying to catch up on the previous week's work and prepare for the week ahead.

Each secretary has an individual style, but all struggle to balance the responsibilities involved and to stop the urgent getting in the way of the important. Those I admired most put great effort into preserving a medium to long-term perspective and fostering a depth of knowledge and analysis to draw on, avoiding the danger of being overly reactive.

This can be done in various ways: having a strong team of able officers, insisting on 'due process', ensuring robust information systems, constantly testing the analysis provided, exhibiting a healthy scepticism and an understanding of practical realities. Usually all of these are required, though the mix will differ with each personality.

Setting priorities is always a challenge. In most portfolios, it is simply impossible to keep on top of the detail, and it is dangerous to try. Equally, however, never delving into details can leave a secretary (and the minister and department) vulnerable when things go wrong. Rolling up the sleeves is, in my view, an essential quality to ensure a minister's priorities are addressed and to demonstrate to staff from time to time the importance of getting the details right.

Establishing priorities also involves taking advantage of cycles. Parliamentary breaks are a useful opportunity to review longer-term strategies. Trips abroad (possibly with the minister) are a time to reflect on policies and performance in the light of international experience. When things go wrong (which happens to all secretaries sometime), it is all hands to the pump, and there is little if any time to reflect on the crisis or to attend to all the other responsibilities not in crisis.

Families inevitably suffer, though most secretaries attempt to set aside some regular period for families, whether through an annual two or three-week holiday, or a Sunday evening dinner, or chauffeuring the children to Saturday morning sport.

Sharing the experience with peers in informal settings also relieves the pressure of work. It is not always possible to discuss issues within the department, or with family and friends, but I have always found having lunch regularly with some other secretaries with whom I share views on the Public Service provides great reassurance. There is a risk, however, that such networks present barriers to newcomers.

Photo acknowledgments

Tony Ayers when Secretary of the Department of Defence (photo by kind permission of the Department of Defence)

Ian Castles when Australian Government Statistician (photo by kind permission of the Australian Bureau of Statistics)

Michael Keating (photo by kind permission of the Department of the Prime Minister and Cabinet)

Helen Williams when Secretary of the Department of Human Services (photo with kind permission of the Department of Human Services)

3. Know the boss: working with and supporting the minister

Elements of this role

Supporting the minister encompasses a range of activities designed to ensure the minister is well informed when making decisions, is well positioned for influencing collective decision making by the government and can be confident that decisions for the portfolio are effectively implemented in the way intended.

The secretary's role involves:

- informing and educating the minister about the department's responsibilities and programs and, indeed, about the processes of government and public service
- communicating to the department the minister's objectives, priorities and preferred style of working, as well as the minister's decisions to be put into effect
- marshalling advice from the department on policy matters, ensuring high quality in terms of analysis, time lines, relevance, understanding of different perspectives and style of presentation
- ensuring timely and quality advice on appointments, grants and other program administration matters requiring ministerial decisions
- overseeing the handling of ministerial correspondence, briefing for Question Time in the Parliament and other briefing (for example, meetings with stakeholders, visits) and the preparation of speech notes, and so on.

In carrying out this role, the secretary needs to build a close, personal relationship with the minister, each understanding the other's style as well as the other's role. They are mutually interdependent.

It is easy for public servants upholding their professional value of being non-partisan and 'apolitical' (a term used in the *Public Service Act*) to underestimate the commitment, skills and idealism of parliamentarians, including those of their own ministers. Without exception, the ministers I served as secretary or while Public Service Commissioner were hardworking and dedicated. I disagreed on occasions with every one of them, but I do not doubt they sincerely believed their positions reflected the public interest tempered by political realities.

Some, like Michael Wooldridge (Minister for Health, 1996–2001) and Brian Howe (Minister for Housing and Regional Development, 1994–96 and Deputy Prime Minister, 1994–95), placed particular emphasis on technical expertise and research evidence in developing their policies. Others, such as John Howard (Prime Minister, 1996–2007), Tony Abbott (Minister Assisting the Prime Minister on the Public Service, 2002–03) and Bronwyn Bishop (Minister for Aged Care, 1998–2001), tended to emphasise their political philosophies. Some, such as Warwick Smith (Minister for Family Services, 1997–98), seemed particularly comfortable with the Public Service, while others, including Howe and Bishop, remained suspicious of the loyalty and competence of public servants who had not yet proved themselves in the minister's eyes.

Working practices also differ. Wooldridge was very comfortable working with email and also liked to ring officers personally for information and advice. Abbott preferred written advice consistent with journalistic practice, with the essential details in the first few paragraphs and with mounting detail so the reader—the minister—could choose to stop at any point without missing something critical. Wooldridge was a 'crammer': he would finalise his position for the Expenditure Review Committee (ERC) in the days and hours before the meeting, well after his formal cabinet submission was distributed, and absorb an astonishing amount of information with an almost photographic memory. Howard also had a remarkable memory for detail, not only for the short term but over months and years.

All the ministers were acutely conscious of the electoral cycle and the need to demonstrate achievements and to be seen to have addressed any significant problems arising on their watch. This is most often the source of tension between politics and administration, as public servants are responsible for bringing to ministers depth and perspective, while politicians must respond to the immediate on anything and everything that might arise, with a close eye on the next election. No minister I served wanted to ignore the longer-term issues, but some, such as Howe and Wooldridge, had more interest in such issues than others; nonetheless, Wooldridge constantly asked for reform ideas with tangible, short-term as well as long-term gains. Abbott also was more willing than his colleagues to address structural reform in health when I was advising the Prime Minister on health services delivery in 2005.

Sometimes, of course, the short-term political pressures simply overwhelm, as happened to Bishop in 2000—despite the real improvements I believe she should be given credit for in the quality and appropriateness of care for older Australians.

Informing and educating the minister

There can be a considerable learning process involved for the minister and the secretary, particularly with a new minister and a new government or with a new secretary. Wooldridge spoke of his first days as a minister finding the Public Service had its own values, with a different language and different ways of operating: it was a different world. He had rarely met any public servants in his time in the House of Representatives and had had no experience of public service processes. He sought advice from people who had been ministers on all sides of politics and was told that after a long period in opposition, a new minister tended to be suspicious. One of the best things he did, he said, was to place on his personal staff a former senior public servant as his chief of staff: 'It was like turning up on a desert island, full of hostile natives and finding someone who spoke my language' (interview in *Health Affairs* 2000). He also adopted some advice he had received from a former senior state public servant to delay detailed briefings from the Public Service—for at least a week—until he had conferred with other key stakeholders, to avoid being perceived to be too dependent on the Public Service from the onset of his ministry. (To my continuing dismay, he publicly endorsed this advice on several occasions over the years, despite being privately highly complimentary about the introductory briefings we provided.)

Table 3.1 Suggestions for working with a new minister

- Establish regular (say, weekly) one-on-one meetings.
- Encourage direct contact between the minister and senior departmental officers, with regular feedback from officers to the secretary re the minister's interests, concerns, styles, and so on.
- Advise the minister of standard cabinet processes, including budget arrangements, consultation processes and central agency roles.
- Advise the minister of standard public service processes and portfolio-specific processes (key legislative requirements, arrangements with states, and so on).
- Clarify the minister's preferred approach to briefing, correspondence and other administrative processes; gain agreement to access the minister's diary.
- Develop regular (say, monthly) one-on-one meetings with the minister's chief of staff to discuss office/departmental relations.

> Ensure clear understanding of allocation of responsibilities among the minister's advisers.
> - Establish a process for a new strategic plan for the department or portfolio, involving the minister directly and also key stakeholders.
> - Open channels of communication with people and organisations the minister draws on (with appropriate sensitivity).
> - Arrange twice-yearly policy review days with the minister involving senior departmental officers and senior advisers, with agreed agenda, short papers and presentations and ample time for discussion.
>
> Source: Drawn in part from advice Ken Baxter has given informally to new ministers on occasion, including Wooldridge in 1996.

The education role is both generic and subject specific. Secretaries bring to the relationship a keen appreciation of the processes of government: the cabinet and budget processes and how the Public Service supports them, the parliamentary and legislative processes, the operations of administrative law and the requirements of financial management. New ministers might not understand these well or at all and a secretary needs to find a diplomatic way to educate the minister and gain his or her confidence in the secretary's advice on due and effective processes.

Ministers expect even new secretaries to know about the department's (and the portfolio's) responsibilities and programs, or at least to ensure the minister has ready access to experience and expertise, which the secretary must be able to complement even in the early days. The secretary is expected quickly to have sufficient knowledge and understanding to add value in discussions about programs and policies, drawing on broader experience of government such as the culture and orientation of central agencies, the perspective of state governments, the time and other practical constraints of legislation and administration. The secretary needs to command the minister's confidence in his/her, and the department's, corporate knowledge and expertise in the subject matter. This can be a particular challenge for a new secretary with a minister who has expertise in the department's area of responsibility (this was particularly the case when Wooldridge, a doctor, was my minister in 1996, but was also true of Howe, an expert in social and town planning, whom I served in the Department of Housing and Regional Development from 1994 to 1996).

Andrew Podger and Michael Wooldridge in the early days of the Department of Health and Family Services (photo by kind permission of the Department of Health and Ageing)

Table 3.2 Learning together

When Michael Wooldridge became Minister for Health and Family Services, I too was new to the portfolio. At his initiative, we engaged in an extensive program of visits and meetings with key people throughout Australia with experience in the portfolio's business, including:

- past ministers from both sides of politics
- leaders of several colleges (GPs, pathologists, radiologists)
- an Australian Medical Association (AMA) leader
- the dean of a medical school
- leaders of key associations (Consumer Health Forum, public health, public hospitals, private hospitals, private health insurance)
- other key individuals in the sector.

It was enormously valuable to each of us and to building the working relationship between us.

With his agreement, I also retained the former secretary, Dr Stephen Duckett, for three months as an adviser to help with the transition,

> including by participating in a series of internal workshops I called to explore issues in each program area.

Communicating to the department

Communicating to the department the requirements of the minister is most important in the initial period with a new minister and/or a new government. It requires knowledge of the party platform, key speeches and statements, but also the Prime Minister's charter letters (Table 3.3) or similar directions and listening closely to the minister and the ministerial staff, understanding the minister's relationship with colleagues and external stakeholders and appreciating broader priorities and philosophies. It involves understanding the particular style of the minister, including the way he or she likes to communicate.

Table 3.3 Charter letters

'Charter letters' from the Prime Minister to ministers became increasingly important under the Howard Government as a formal framework for keeping the government focused on its political priorities. Surprisingly, given Prime Minister Kevin Rudd's reputation for bureaucratic processes and early advice that he would continue the practice, charter letters have not been issued yet under the Rudd Government.

Each minister received a detailed letter from the Prime Minister at the beginning of each term of office setting out the Prime Minister's expectations and priorities. The letters complemented the Administrative Arrangements Order, which is the legal instrument setting out the principal matters dealt with by departments and portfolio ministers, and identified for each minister (whether a portfolio minister or not) the particular priorities the Prime Minister wished him or her to pursue in the next three years. The letters effectively identified the respective responsibilities of the portfolio minister and any junior ministers, though details might be left to the portfolio minister to settle (including the responsibilities of any parliamentary secretary).

The letters incorporated election commitments, but went further to specify broader policy directions and particular targets, whether or not in the publicly available policy platform. The letters were held very tightly, copied only to the secretary, who might provide access only to relevant excerpts to senior officers who needed to know.

The letters grew over the years (increasing, as I recall, from three to four pages in 1996 to 10 or more pages in later years), and the process for reporting progress against them became more formal. In the first term of the Howard Government, Wooldridge chose not to report progress in writing but to see the Prime Minister from time to time to discuss directions and priorities. Later, he started to provide written reports (but not every year) drawing on notes I would provide to his office. I did not see his final reports.

Maintaining the system of letters and reports became increasingly formal and bureaucratic and few ministers would risk not reporting in writing to Prime Minister Howard and most would rely heavily on drafting by the secretary.

The charter letters, while highly confidential with very limited circulation, affected the priorities of secretaries as well as ministers. They played a major role in shaping portfolio budget submissions and also affected departmental strategic plans and processes.

Ensuring a large department is fully appreciative of the minister's requirements can take up to a year or more with a new government: it is easy for even senior public servants to fail to appreciate the extent to which their processes and styles have become attuned to the previous regime after a long term of government.

Marshalling advice

Policy advising, and marshalling policy advice from the department, is a central responsibility of a secretary of an Australian government department. It might not be as critical at state level, where the emphasis is often more on management and service delivery. The secretary is expected always to add value, whether by his or her own analytical capacity and knowledge of the department's business or by bringing to bear judgments from long experience and knowledge of the likely views of key players and the Australian public. The secretary must also ensure the necessary capability in the department in terms of skilled people, retrievable data, research and evaluation, access to external expertise and information, and internal communications and processes that bring the necessary skills and information together when needed (see Chapter 6).

I usually gave division heads (and indeed branch heads, and often section heads, who were frequently identified on minutes as the 'contact officer') considerable authority to offer policy advice, while expecting them to liaise with other interested divisions and portfolio agencies before doing so. The deputy secretaries and I would normally have been engaged in the earlier deliberations, but did not often sign off on the minute or brief. Exceptions included budget matters on which I always took the lead personally. I expected advice to offer options, but give a clear, preferred position. On rare occasions, I sent the minister a supplementary note giving a different view from that put forward by a division head. This occurred several times in 1996 when the new government was still developing its position on many matters and I was also new: I wanted to test the views of several divisions but felt the government was best served by hearing from them as well as me. The main occasions this occurred concerned child care, where I was challenging the efficiency and equity of service subsidies over cash assistance direct to families with young children, and I was seeking to clarify the new government's philosophy towards competition in the childcare industry. (As it turned out, the government took the division's more conservative approach.)

I was always personally involved in any significant policy development, as well as marshalling the advice of responsible officers in the department. This usually went beyond participation in departmental deliberations to guiding the direction of the policy advice, whether in housing reform, urban development, Aboriginal health, primary health care or private health insurance.

Part of the value adding I always tried to provide was to ensure the policy advice fitted well with the broader and longer-term context. This imposed considerable discipline, including awareness of international and academic work, consideration of longer-term reform strategies and understanding of the government's wider economic and social policies. It also helped to identify opportunities that a narrower approach might have missed.

Table 3.4 Child immunisation

Minister Wooldridge should be given great credit for successfully addressing the alarming drop in child immunisation rates in the period to 1996. Through careful highlighting of individual cases of deaths from failure to immunise children against measles in particular, he turned our bland statistics of falling immunisation rates into headline stories of personal tragedies and a sense of crisis that had to be addressed.

Our role was to help the minister identify options to reverse the trend. In late 1996 and early 1997, we explored a range of measures involving sticks and carrots, some involving our portfolio's programs and others involving other portfolios' programs. The main carrots involved rewards for GPs if a high proportion of their young patients were immunised, while the main sticks were the placement of conditions on access to maternity benefits and childcare subsidies relating to the children's immunisation.

The political crisis fostered by Wooldridge made the Prime Minister and other ministers sympathetic to the measures proposed, which were agreed to by cabinet in early 1997. The measures achieved remarkable success, returning immunisation rates to previous high levels (and higher), well

---

exceeding the critical 'herd protection' levels needed against the communicable diseases involved.

The rewards for GPs were also consistent with our longer-term strategy to shift the funding of GPs towards 'blended payments', away from pure fee-for-service, to increase financial incentives for quality care and health outcomes rather than just throughput.

It was always important also to be ready for opportunities to press policy initiatives. Much has been written about 'policy cycles', from decisions to implementation to evaluation and advice, contributing to new decisions. That is a useful normative approach emphasising the importance of systematic review and evaluation, but it is not an accurate description of real practice. Political decisions are taken when opportunities arise. Departments and secretaries need to have a store of good policy ideas to put to ministers at opportune times. Wooldridge certainly appreciated this, for example, when we had well-developed proposals to put forward when the Howard Government was looking for a rural package after the Rural Summit. He has since told me he regards this as among his major successes that will stand the test of time.

Notwithstanding the time pressures on them, ministers generally are keen to ensure their policy decisions are well founded and their policies are likely to have a long-term beneficial impact on Australian society. Howe looked to external policy analysts who had his confidence, such as Meredith Edwards and Jenny Macklin (and Bettina Cass in earlier years), to undertake major policy reviews. When I became secretary of his department, I was aware of his lack of confidence in the housing division I inherited from his former mega-department and I put considerable effort into strengthening its capacity while personally directing the policy development process, drawing on my earlier expertise in social security. I was not as positive as he was about the National Housing Strategy review he initiated before my time, but I did accept we had to improve our policy advising performance, which we did (Table 4.5).

Wooldridge was less enamoured of external reviews and we established an arrangement whereby at least once a year we would set aside a full day for discussions on long-term policy directions, led by short presentations by senior departmental officers highlighting trends and evaluations, and raising longer-term policy options. These canvassed, for example, increasing Commonwealth leadership in health, including possible full financial takeover, restructuring the regulation of private health insurance, broadening the base of primary health care and strengthening cost-effectiveness criteria for government health benefits.

Supporting the minister's administrative responsibilities

Supporting the minister in meeting his or her administrative responsibilities such as appointments and grants also requires good internal processes reflecting the requirements of administrative law and program legislation and an appreciation of the public interest in the principles of merit, value for money, fairness and ethics. Ministers might have considerable discretion in such decision making and secretaries have a vital role in helping them to exercise that discretion in a well-informed way. This involves building the necessary culture of responsiveness to the minister and appreciation of the public interest, and having the necessary processes in the department.

Ministerial correspondence and briefs

Secretaries cannot afford to rely entirely on others to manage ministerial correspondence, Question Time briefs, and so on. These directly affect how a minister is seen to be performing among fellow MPs (including rivals for the ministry and rivals for the government), the Parliamentary Press Gallery and with the public, including the minister's constituents. The secretary needs to be sure of the people and processes involved and to have constant monitoring of the department's performance with regular reports to the secretary and executive (see also Chapter 10).

Variations in the balance of roles

The role of a secretary in supporting the minister will vary according to the size and function of the department and the styles of the secretary and minister.

A large department inevitably limits the hands-on role of a secretary and adds to the coordination and oversight role. In time, this places more emphasis on internal departmental processes, systems and communications. A department with a predominantly policy role will usually involve more direct links between the secretary and minister, while one with more service delivery responsibilities might involve less direct contact. (Interestingly, however, this is not reflected in state government practice where, notwithstanding the greater service delivery role, ministers and secretaries commonly have adjacent offices; the establishment of the Human Services portfolio by the Commonwealth might also signal increasing ministerial interest in service delivery as well as policy.)

Secretaries have to accommodate the different styles of ministers. Some ministers have a very close interest in the operations of the department, while others are more closely focused on higher levels of political interaction, in cabinet, the party and the Parliament. Brian Howe, despite being Deputy Prime Minister, spoke firmly to me about his constitutional responsibility 'to administer' the department (the *Constitution*, s. 64). On the other hand, Robert Ray, then Minister for Defence, made it clear he did not need me to bother him on issues of management that did not require his personal involvement. Most of my ministers were more in Ray's than Howe's style.

Some secretaries enjoy the buzz of the political environment and some of these provide a lot of immediate support during current pressures, which ministers greatly appreciate (though I disapprove of secretaries confusing their role and that of ministerial staff by constantly visiting or even working from the minister's office). Others prefer to marshal the necessary support mostly from a little distance, allowing them to draw on their particular public service strengths in terms of longer-term considerations or wider and deeper analysis. Neither approach is necessarily good or bad, as long as secretaries have in place processes to complement their own styles and strengths and are able to adjust their styles for different circumstances. My own style was more in line with the latter approach, allowing me (I felt) to give weight to the longer-term public interest, but at times it did lead to vulnerability when political crises developed that required more immediate and direct support.

Changes in the role over time

The communications revolution and the increased power and pervasiveness of the media, along with global competitive pressures, have had a profound effect on the role of secretaries in supporting ministers. This effect can be seen in many developments:

- the 24/7 focus on politics and the increased capacity required by ministers to respond and manage the immediate demands of the media
- the increased expectation on government by the public, including immediacy of action, the linking of all program activities and the almost limitless reach of government
- the response by governments of greater central control and control of communications in particular
- the increased role of ministerial staff
- the increased involvement in policy and administration by non-governmental organisations and individuals.

To some extent, this has introduced more competition to policy advising as well as program administration, keeping secretaries and their officers on their toes. It has also affected the way secretaries go about supporting their ministers:

- working very often with the ministerial staff, relying less on direct dealings with the minister
- building more extensive external relationships, with interest groups and think tanks in particular

- establishing more sophisticated communications capacity within the department, closely linked to the minister's office, and with closer control of external communications and relations with the media.

For these reasons, I have included a separate chapter (10) on communications and dealing with the media, while also describing aspects of the impact on secretaries in this chapter and the chapter (6) on management.

Increased management responsibilities through the financial and personnel management reforms of the 1980s and 1990s have also inevitably demanded more of secretaries' own time adding to ministers' tendencies to draw on the advice of ministerial staff and external groups, and to the need for secretaries and departments to build close links with advisers and external groups.

Another change since 1987 has been the introduction of portfolio ministers with junior ministers as well as parliamentary secretaries (who are also, in effect, junior ministers). Secretaries might now have three or more ministers to support, requiring them to rely more heavily on deputy secretaries, with ministers in turn relying more heavily also on their ministerial staff.

Table 3.5 The 'ministerial team'

We always referred to the group of ministers and parliamentary secretaries as 'the ministerial team'. The term was without exception somewhat of an oxymoron. The competition between ministers is always a central factor to take into account.

When Brian Howe was the Minister for Housing and Regional Development (1994–96), we had strict instructions not to copy our advice to him to the parliamentary secretary, Mary Crawford. Howe's advisers were particularly keen to exclude her entirely from involvement in the regional economic development program despite her nominal responsibility for local government, which was critical to the program.

When Michael Wooldridge was Minister for Health and Family Services (1996–98), relations between the ministers seemed generally positive, but I always felt sympathy for Judi Moylan, who had to carry responsibility for the 1996 cuts to aged care and child care with little public support from the senior minister and his ERC colleagues who were the decision makers. (I remain of the view that the measures were generally worthwhile not only because they addressed the immediate budget pressures but because of their longer-term benefits.) Moylan was replaced by Warwick Smith before the 1998 election (when he lost his seat).

Later, when Wooldridge was Minister for Health and Aged Care and Bronwyn Bishop was the Minister for Aged Care (1998–2001), the relationship could be more difficult. For example, early in the 1999 budget process, there was a joint meeting with Bishop and the then Parliamentary Secretary, Senator Grant Tambling, to discuss portfolio priorities. This did not go well and subsequently the interaction on budget matters was between each minister and the department, with the department relaying to each the views and directions of the others (no doubt complemented by interaction between the respective ministerial offices).

My practice in the Health department was to identify a particular deputy to provide most of the secretary-equivalent support to each junior minister, while making it clear any minister had the right to deal with me directly if they needed (or preferred) to. I retained the central role with the portfolio minister. For the most part, this worked well, each minister feeling he or she received the attention required and the department being in a good position to coordinate and to ensure the portfolio minister could be kept informed across the full range of responsibilities. The arrangement also allowed the deputies to learn more about the role of a secretary in serving a minister.

On one or two occasions, Bishop expressed the view that I was not providing sufficient personal support to her as I was too occupied with supporting the portfolio minister, but she was certainly always complimentary about the dedicated support she received from the deputy secretary, Mary Murnane. Parliamentary secretaries such as Trish Worth and Grant Tambling also always told me they were very satisfied with the support they received from deputies Ian Lindenmayer and David Borthwick, respectively.

Current issues and challenges

Some issues surrounding the support of ministers by secretaries never change: getting the balance right between responsiveness to the elected government and its minister and apolitical professionalism in the public interest has always been a challenge and a matter for judgment. Both are essential, but pursuing one to the extent of compromising the other is not appropriate.

Some secretaries in the late 1990s referred to their ministers as their departments' 'primary customers' in their strategic plans and other exhortations to staff. I always firmly rejected that view, not only because it misrepresented the accountability framework in government, but because it promoted excessive responsiveness and even obsequiousness to ministers. If private sector analogies must be used, a minister is more like the chairman of the board and the secretary more like the CEO. The CEO is responsible to the board, which agrees on the strategic direction of the organisation, including who is the primary customer and how the organisation is to serve them. For government departments, the 'primary customer' was the Australian public, and I used our strategic planning to ensure ministerial endorsement of the way we intended to serve the public.

In my experience, there is rarely much controversy in providing policy advice to ministers. Most ministers are keen to be presented with options and do not object to advice advocating an option they do not support (though inexperienced ministerial advisers do sometimes try to constrain such advice). The challenge is more acute when the advice concerns an issue of due process: a freedom-of-information (FOI) request, information to be included in an annual report, the need for a competitive tender process or other constraint about a grant or contract. In this situation, a secretary might consider there is no room for offering options: there is only due process. The minister may still reject the advice (if it is lawful to do so) because of immediate political embarrassment, but most know that in doing so their future political risks might be heightened. The advice on due process is itself sometimes regarded as the problem and the provision of such 'frank and fearless' advice requires the most courage, in my experience.

Table 3.6 Whose annual report?

Annual reports set out departmental performance against the targets set out in the portfolio budget statements for that year.

In the draft 2000–01 annual report, we included data on the number of occupied aged-care places compared with the targets set out in the portfolio budget statements: there was a small shortfall. This was of considerable concern to Minister Bishop, who had been responding to sustained criticism of insufficient places by announcing new funding for more places. Her statements, including approved places not yet occupied, demonstrated a commitment to considerable expansion, but the annual report would show that we had not yet met the government's own target in terms of occupied places.

Following usual practice, I had provided copies of the draft report to ministers well in advance to allow time for comment. After some initial response, I agreed to include in the report figures on approved places showing that new investments were being made, but insisted that the data and comparisons based on occupied places remain.

As the deadline approached for publishing to meet parliamentary obligations, I advised Minister Bishop's office that I needed to proceed that weekend. Bishop rang me, directing very forcefully that nothing was to go to the printer until she had approved the wording, which was not possible for another week as she was travelling to Central Australia. It was her report, she said, and it would not include data that were not in her public statements. I gently reminded her that it was in fact my report, that I was obliged to report against the published portfolio budget statements targets and that Parliament had set the deadlines.

Nonetheless, we held back the printing to the last possible minute. Deputy Secretary Mary Murnane spent several hours with the minister in Alice Springs going through the draft in minute detail and I agreed to a few minor amendments while retaining the key data. The report was eventually tabled (after further resistance from the minister when the 2001 election was called).

The challenge to balance responsiveness and impartial professionalism is not always about resisting excessive pressure for responsiveness. In the early days of a new government, the challenge is frequently in the reverse direction: departments can be slow to understand the priorities and styles of the new minister and government and considerable attention has to be given to providing ministers with the opportunity to exercise the authority they have earned and to change policies, procedures, priorities and resource allocation. Wooldridge has told me he felt some areas of the department continued to pursue their own agendas and were slow to respond to his decisions when they did not align with their views (there might have been some truth to this and there were cases where I intervened to press for quicker and more positive responses, but some of the concerns of the relevant officers reflected statutory responsibilities not personal agendas and certainly did warrant testing of the minister's directions).

Officers can also sometimes move into 'caretaker mode' too early, resisting acting on minister's political decisions before an election has been called. I always took the view that three-year terms were already very short and the public interest would not be served at all if the Public Service effectively shortened these terms. There are clear rules as to when the caretaker period begins and until that time ministers have every right to expect their lawful instructions to be obeyed. Of course, the nearer governments get to elections, the more often poor decisions tend to be made, and the more important good and frank advice can be.

More recent issues include working with substantial ministerial offices and handling the closer control of government communications.

Ministerial staffers are a critical part of the political landscape in Australia, reflecting an international trend in government. They not only provide important politically oriented support to the minister, in doing so, they can take pressure off 'politicising' the Public Service through partisan appointments or activities. These advantages can be jeopardised if the advisers overstep the mark in their relations with public servants.

Table 3.7 Building trust with ministerial staff

Good relations with the minister's staff are important but not always easy. I learned from my early experience with Brian Howe's staff that, as secretary, I needed to invest more of my own time in the relationship.

I had some concerns about his staff relating in particular to the level of intervention down into my (small) department and the lack of clarity about responsibilities in the office (indeed, there was frequently disagreement among his staff and competition to gain his ear). Given the chief of staff seemed to have limited authority over the other advisers, I chose to raise my concerns with the minister himself, but only after I felt confident of our own performance in serving him and addressing his policy priorities. This proved at least partially successful (see also Chapter 7), but ran the risk of openly challenging people with a very longstanding and close personal relationship with the minister.

With Michael Wooldridge's office, I used a different tack, which I think is generally the better one. I worked hard on my own relationship with the chief of staff, Barbara Hayes (and later Ken Smith). We arranged to meet every month or so over a glass of wine in my office. We would each draw up an agenda, which, while dominated by issues of policy or program substance, usually included a few incidents between the department and office causing one or other (or both) of us concern. The informality allowed us to talk frankly about the department's performance or an adviser's overstepping the mark, including incidents involving either of us personally. It did not resolve everything, but it diffused many situations that might otherwise have escalated into a brawl requiring ministerial involvement.

Control of communications similarly can present a two-edged sword. Good control can help build confidence in the relationship between ministers and the Public Service (nothing so quickly destroys trust as leaks or other failures in communications management). Excessive control, however, can inhibit the release or even the preparation of information, such as research and statistics, which is in the public interest.

Trust, relations and confidence are put under greatest pressure during political crises. I have experienced my fair share, learning the importance of keeping open channels of communication with the minister and office while taking responsibility for project management of the crisis within the department, ensuring timely collection of information, preparation of useful briefs, and so on. I was not always successful in this (Table 3.8).

Table 3.8 Managing political crises: the 'scan scam' and kerosene baths

The years 1999 and 2000 were particularly difficult for me and the department, as well as for my two ministers, Michael Wooldridge and Bronwyn Bishop. Administrative weaknesses in the department contributed to incidents that spiralled into political crises colloquially known as the 'scan scam' and the kerosene baths case. Years later, I might be able to convince some people that, in both cases, despite the immediate failures, the underlying programs and initiatives were achieving substantial improvements in the quality of care, and in a cost-effective way. At the time, however, we were all in the bunker under continuous attack by the media, interest groups and the Opposition.

An interesting side to this was the different approaches taken to managing the two crises—one effective, the other not.

During the magnetic resonance imaging (MRI) crisis in 1999, we established a small team in the department to coordinate support for Wooldridge. The team met in my office briefly each morning and we would have a short teleconference with the minister's chief of staff to discuss the latest media stories, the information needed to respond, the likely tactics in Parliament (for example, Question Time, Matter of Public Importance debate, censure motion). My officers would then seek out the necessary information and draft some briefs. Late in the morning, we would meet again in my office, go through the material, send it to the minister's office and have a further teleconference to test if we had covered what was needed and to discuss further the tactics the minister might prepare for. The minister's office would then take over control, turning the briefs into speeches and so on, liaising with the Prime Minister's Office and the minister representing in the Senate. Most days, I spoke to the minister late in the day to review the situation.

For a time, relations between the minister's office and the department were understandably fraught, but I rang the chief of staff advising him that whatever their criticisms of the department, the minister and I (and he) needed to keep the lines of communication between us open, every day. This we did, and it helped enormously.

The aged-care crisis in 2000 was inherently more complex (new claims were being aired about nursing homes around Australia each day), but it still was not managed nearly as well as it should have been. First, despite my objections, the head of the Department of the Prime Minister and Cabinet, Max Moore-Wilton, instructed me to work from Bishop's office. This confused my role and the office's role. We set up a team in the department under the deputy, but control there was made more difficult by pressure on me to intervene continuously when briefings were late. Briefings were constantly late, as we attempted to get the facts on every claim from around Australia by lunchtime, rather than prioritise and insist on extra time to investigate details. The department was also struggling to get its state offices to appreciate the importance of the crisis and their responsibility to respond more quickly and clearly.

The office was not operating smoothly either, with the Prime Minister's Office constantly intruding to criticise the department ('You need a baseball bat, Andrew, to take to the department') and insufficient attention was paid to ensuring the minister representing Bishop in the Senate (Amanda Vanstone) was properly briefed. Support from the portfolio minister's office was offered but not taken up. Everything was done on the run, with much blame and insufficient cooperation.

The only one I felt could hold their head up for performing well was the deputy secretary, Mary Murnane, who was calm in the crisis and accepted the second-best management approach, performing as leader of the team back in the department and at times providing some of the personal support for the minister that should have come from the office.

Postscript: some light relief

Twice during the kerosene baths crisis, while in difficult meetings with Bishop and her advisers, I was called away to answer an urgent phone call from the portfolio minister, Wooldridge. While each time there was some point of substance to the call, the main purpose was: 'I thought you might need a break, Andrew.'

Lessons for successfully supporting the minister

Among the lessons from my own experience are the following.

- Notwithstanding the benefits of supporting processes and mechanisms, the secretary must have regular, direct contact with the minister, initiating that contact as well as responding to requests.
- Where there is more than one minister in the portfolio, it is helpful to assign a deputy to each junior minister or parliamentary secretary, to provide dedicated support. This does not entirely replace the need for the portfolio secretary to be available to support the non-portfolio ministers, but it does spread the load effectively and meets most requirements for secretary-level support.
- Ministers rely heavily on secretaries for advice on due process. In the early days, some diplomatic teaching of a minister by a secretary is required.

Courage might be needed at times in giving advice on due process, but most ministers appreciate it in the longer term.

- Secretaries are also almost always expected to be able to add value to policy advice. This does not require constraining advice from departmental experts, but guiding that advice and helping to identify alternative options and take into account wider issues and context.

- Strategic planning, directly involving ministers, can help build the necessary relationship. Strategic plans focus on 'why' and 'how', complementing policy platforms, charter letters and portfolio budget statements that determine 'what' achievements are expected and the resources involved. They can be regarded as high-level agreements between the minister and the department and should be formally endorsed by the minister. The minister is never, however, the department's 'primary customer'; the minister is the boss.

- Setting a day aside, at least once a year, for high-level discussions with the minister on longer-term policy issues and directions is enormously helpful in ensuring policy coherence and understanding of the evidence behind the department's policy advice.

- While never replacing direct meetings, emails and phone calls with the minister, the secretary should arrange regular meetings with the minister's chief of staff. Informal discussions covering agendas drawn up by both parties can help to diffuse misunderstandings, focus attention on matters of importance to the minister and clarify the basis of 'frank and fearless' advice that might be causing unease.

- Such contacts are even more important in times of political crisis when there might be tension between the minister and the department.

- Encouraging the chief of staff to clarify the division of responsibilities among ministerial staff can serve to limit miscommunications between the department and the office and to enhance the relevance and timeliness of advice.

- Departmental liaison officers should be high-performing officers with a lot of potential for more senior roles in the future. This demonstrates to the minister and ministerial staff the calibre of public servants in the department, reduces the risk of an 'us and them' mentality developing and provides excellent training opportunities for future public service executives.

Photo acknowledgments

Michael Wooldridge when Minister for Health and Family Services (photo by kind permission of the Parliamentary Library)
Brian Howe when Deputy Prime Minister and Minister for Housing and Regional Development (photo by kind permission of the Parliamentary Library)

4. Know the real boss: support to the Prime Minister and the whole of government

Left: Prime Minister Paul Keating who first appointed Podger as Secretary of the Department of Administrative Services and the Arts in December 1993 (photo with kind permission of the Parliamentary Library)

Right: Prime Minister John Howard who appointed Podger as Secretary of the Department of Health and Family Services in March 1996, renewing the appointment as Secretary of the Department of Health and Aged Care in 2001, and appointing Podger as Public Service Commissioner from 2002 (photo by kind permission of the Parliamentary Library)

Elements of the role

The contribution of secretaries to 'collective responsibility' involves a number of activities, which overlap and link with the activities involved in supporting the minister. These include:

- involvement with cabinet and cabinet committees such as the Expenditure Review Committee (ERC)
- contributing to cross-portfolio policy development and review
- participating in meetings of secretaries, particularly meetings chaired by the Secretary of the Department of the Prime Minister and Cabinet (PM&C).

In addition, there has been an increasing role for formal guidance from the Prime Minister to ministers on political priorities over a term of office. As described in Chapter 3, charter letters grew in importance, length and formality during the Howard years; while Prime Minister Rudd has not so far continued that practice, he is certainly no less interventionist in his style, placing strong emphasis on whole-of-government management and political control.

It was common practice under the Hawke, Keating and Howard Governments for officials to attend cabinet committee meetings (though not cabinet itself) and to be invited to contribute to the discussion. The Rudd Government has continued the practice. This has proven to be an effective way of ensuring informed and timely consideration of the issues by ministers. Ministers can choose not to have officials accompany them or to have the relevant policy expert, who is not the secretary (this apparently is less common under the Rudd Government). Unless I felt insufficiently knowledgeable on the matters under consideration, I usually sought to be the official involved, as I was most often able to relate the issues concerned to wider policies and experience. I also had more experience than most of how cabinet committees worked, having sat on the ERC for many years in the Department of Finance and provided briefings to the Prime Minister when in PM&C.

Table 4.1 Doing deals in the ERC

In the 1995 budget process, Brian Howe was having difficulty getting support from his colleagues for his vision of a continuing role for the Commonwealth in cities and regions. The Prime Minister, Paul Keating, was sympathetic, particularly about the Better Cities program: he suggested the final decision on its funding be deferred until the inner cabinet could reflect on the revenue available at the end of the budget process. Howe, however, needed not only to keep his proposal for that program alive, he needed to avoid the ERC rejecting everything else on the table in order to offset what some ERC members clearly considered an indulgence of the Prime Minister and his deputy.

Howe's budget proposals covered a range of housing programs as well as cities and regional development. The standard ERC rule was that genuine, continuing savings must offset new policy. Howe's proposal did not meet this requirement and certainly did not provide savings to offset any post-ERC decision to provide new capital funds for cities.

The ERC gave Howe a hard time and he and his adviser (who attended with me) were dejected, as it seemed nothing would go the minister's way. I was, however, conscious that one of the minister's proposals was not really a priority for the portfolio (it was included at the strong insistence of another adviser) and, indeed, I suspected we would not spend the allocation we already had for that program. I quietly asked Howe if I could propose a deal, offering not only to withdraw that proposal but to offer up some savings. He agreed with reluctance, assuming there was no hope of a useful decision. I put the idea to the Finance Minister, Kim Beazley, as a trade for all the other proposals except for Better Cities, which was to be deferred until later anyway. Beazley turned to Prime Minister Keating, who was about to close the meeting on a sour note, to say that perhaps a deal was possible after all. Howe indicated he would accept my suggestion, which Beazley recommended to the ERC.

Howe and his adviser were still despondent. They had not appreciated the significance of the deal, having heard only that no new money was yet agreed for Better Cities, that another proposed measure had gone backwards and only criticism of the portfolio and Howe's vision.

It was not until the ERC cabinet decision was circulated that the minister and his office realised what we had won. Written cabinet decisions always reflect the exact words in the minister's cabinet submission unless cabinet (or the ERC) specifically decides differently. Thus, every proposal was endorsed exactly as recommended with just two exceptions, and we had been extremely careful with the drafting of the minister's submission. On Better Cities, the decision included the minister's vision for the program, including that it would be a continuing one, but deferred the amount of new capital to be provided each year.

Belatedly, there was some celebration, particularly when new funds for Better Cities were also subsequently agreed.

The celebration was short-lived, as the department and the Better Cities program were abolished a year later.

For most of my time as a secretary, my minister was a member of the ERC. This can be an enormous advantage if well managed. The minister may seek departmental advice on submissions from other portfolios. When this happened, I usually did my best to provide the advice myself or drew on one or two senior officers with relevant experience. I provided Howe with advice on superannuation and tax (finding, to the Treasury's embarrassment, significant errors in its 1995 cabinet documents) and Wooldridge with advice on education, social security, housing and defence in 1996 and 1997, with substantial assistance from Louise Morauta, another former finance officer. Wooldridge took his broader ERC responsibilities very seriously and his performance was well regarded, including by Finance and Treasury department officials. This helped him when his own portfolio was under review, though more in terms of understanding the 'rules of the game' than in getting any special treatment.

Table 4.2 Clearing officials from the cabinet room

Very early in 1996, Michael Wooldridge asked me how the ERC worked. I outlined the process, emphasising that it was open to the (new) Prime Minister to vary it as he wished. The minister asked in particular whether he could ask for a ministers-only discussion to canvass political aspects without officials present. I told him that was a matter he could raise with the chair, usually being the Prime Minister when health was being discussed, noting nonetheless the advantages of having officials present.

Wooldridge frequently pursued this, seeking an opportunity for ministers-only discussions after some initial debate on his budget proposals with officials present. Max Moore-Wilton in particular was not amused, for the good reasons that the debate might not be as well-informed if central agency officials were not there to question arguments presented as facts and that the cabinet decision drafted by officials subsequently might not fully reflect the subtleties of the discussion and its conclusions.

Possibly for these very reasons, Wooldridge felt the idea served him well, strengthening his capacity to win his arguments. I advised him a few years later that he was using the tactic too often and was putting at risk his relationship with the Prime Minister, who was receiving strong objections from Moore-Wilton. He told me that he accepted my advice just before another ERC meeting. Nonetheless, about half an hour into the meeting, he turned to the Prime Minister and asked for a ministers-only discussion. It was a spur-of-the-moment request and was agreed to by the Prime Minister. Moore-Wilton glared down the table at the minister and me as he rose to leave. As I also rose, the minister said quietly to me: 'I got that wrong, didn't I?'

Contributing to the cabinet process also entails substantial prior work with other agencies and, frequently, post-cabinet work. Interaction with other agencies often contributed to the design of the minister's proposals and identified the key issues for debate in the cabinet room. This is articulated formally in the coordination comments in the minister's submission to cabinet and in the Department of Finance 'Green' (the Finance department's briefing for the ERC or cabinet ministers on each submission coming forward that has resource implications). Post-cabinet work can involve bilateral or trilateral deliberation to resolve differences consistent with cabinet directions or to explore additional options or to test proposals in more detail. It also involves providing regular reports to the Cabinet Implementation Unit and responses to questions raised about implementation.

Secretaries' personal involvement in such work depends on the significance of the issues involved. It is not unusual for secretary-to-secretary discussions to resolve, or at least narrow, differences for ministerial decisions. Most of the interaction among officials, however, occurs among SES officers, and sometimes below the SES. Particularly in any post-cabinet work, it is common that the respective ministerial offices will confer to resolve matters that cannot be settled by secretaries or other officials, or to identify politically acceptable compromises. In the pre-cabinet stages, there could also be some liaison between ministerial offices, parallel to the interaction among officials, exploring the political dimensions of the different views of the portfolios.

There are many mechanisms for whole-of-government policy development and management. The advantages and disadvantages of different processes and structures are canvassed in the 2004 Management Advisory Committee report *Connected Government*. Secretaries' involvement in such cross-portfolio activities is usually at the initial stages in setting the terms of reference for an exercise and at the final stages in confirming each department's position on the emerging policy options, proposals and conclusions. It is also increasingly common for a reference group of secretaries, often chaired by the Secretary of the Department of PM&C, to oversee the work of a task force or interdepartmental committee, to ensure it is developing options that address the agenda ministers have set and that are achievable in the desired time frame. This was the model used effectively when I chaired the Prime Minister's Task Force on Health Services Delivery in 2005.

Secretaries (and their officers) are usually required to wear two hats in these exercises. The first is in line with their statutory duty to work 'under the minister', representing the minister's views and the department's program interests. The second is to collaborate to help achieve a collective solution for the Prime Minister and the government.

Table 4.3 Task Force on Health Services Delivery

From late 2004 until mid-2005, I chaired a task force on the delivery of health services in Australia. I had a small team of very able officers, seconded from the departments of Health and Ageing, Treasury and the Prime Minister and Cabinet, working for me. We were based in the Department of the Prime Minister and Cabinet.

There was also a reference group of the secretaries from these three departments, ensuring the task force addressed the terms of reference and met the objectives of the Prime Minister. The reference group commented on outlines and drafts of the report and took responsibility for a covering cabinet memorandum to which the final report was attached. Members of the Prime Minister's Office (PMO) attended most meetings of the reference group.

The report was nonetheless my report and I took very seriously my professional independence in preparing it (though I was directed not to consult widely). I resisted the preference of the Department of PM&C and the PMO to focus on incremental reform, believing that the terms of reference and the context in which the task force was established required me to give equal if not more attention to options for longer-term reform.

I was given the opportunity to brief the Prime Minister directly on the report and subsequently to brief the cabinet. They endorsed most of my shorter-term proposals, but baulked at my options for more fundamental reform.

I believe the structure of the exercise was a very good one and am only disappointed by the government's decision not to publish the final report.

The Secretary of the Department of PM&C chairs a monthly meeting of portfolio secretaries plus the Public Service Commissioner. These meetings are usually of one hour's duration and focus mostly on informing secretaries of the current policy priorities of the Prime Minister and senior ministers, and processes for handling these and other high-level matters. Sometimes particular policy issues are discussed but, in the short time available, such discussion usually focuses on identifying a suitable process for more considered study and advice to ministers within the relevant timetable. Public service management issues are also sometimes identified but, again, mostly with a view to establishing a process for more considered study.

Once a year, the Secretary of the Department of PM&C hosts a two-day retreat that allows more substantial discussion of selected emerging policy issues and of some management issues (I understand, however, there was no retreat in 2008). As a rule, the Prime Minister joins the group for a lengthy discussion of his priorities and strategies and of any concerns secretaries might wish to raise. These discussions were usually very useful, Prime Minister Howard being quite forthcoming and frank in his assessments of future policy directions on such diverse issues as privatisation, Indigenous welfare and demographic change. On occasions, however, some secretaries seemed to use the opportunity to promote themselves rather than informed and frank discussion.

Table 4.4 Bring back the biff

At one portfolio secretaries' retreat, there was a more robust discussion than usual among secretaries and other invited agency heads of the government's policy on information technology (IT) outsourcing. Several people argued against the mandating of such outsourcing—the Statistician, Bill McLennan, being perhaps the most outspoken. While not constraining the discussion on this occasion, Max Moore-Wilton questioned McLennan's insistence on his statutory independence and hence his ability to ignore the government's policy.

McLennan, a former ACT rugby front rower, finally had enough. 'If you say that again, Max, I'll biff you one.'

It was a most effective way of getting his argument listened to seriously by Moore-Wilton—better than my tendency to be quietly persistent or some others' tendency just to go quiet.

Apart from these formal and regular gatherings (and those focused specifically on APS management—see Chapter 10), secretaries often meet in smaller forums, often informally, to confer on issues of shared interest. When Secretary of the Health department, I continued the practice (mentioned in Chapter 2) of Tony Blunn, former Secretary of the Department of Social Security, of hosting monthly lunches of the secretaries of the social policy departments. The heads of other related agencies such as Centrelink also became involved and the value of the gatherings proved so great to those participating that secretaries refused to drop off the invitation list when they moved away from the social policy area. As a result, the attendance at times was counterproductive to the private discussions intended.

As well as such informal forums, there is often the need for selected secretaries to meet to discuss a matter of shared interest to their ministers and to establish processes through which officials can explore the issue in more detail. Examples in the Housing department included work with the departments of Social Security and PM&C (and later The Treasury and the Finance department) on housing reform and rental assistance and with the departments of Employment and Transport on regional development and cities; examples in the Department of Health included work with the Industry department on pharmaceutical pricing and regulation, with the Department of Veterans' Affairs on medical and pharmaceutical benefits, aged care and patient health records, with the Department of Family and Community Services on rehabilitation and health assessment services for social security clients, and with Customs, the Attorney-General's Department and others on illicit drug strategies.

Variations on these roles and activities

The extent of whole-of-government activity depends critically on the function of the department. Some departments are inevitably involved constantly in whole-of-government activities: the central agencies themselves and other agencies with specific coordinating roles (for example, the Attorney-General's and Foreign Affairs departments). Departments with wide responsibilities, such as the Health department, also find themselves with substantial overlapping interests with other agencies.

The extent also varies with the style and interests of the Prime Minister and the Secretary of the Department of PM&C. Prime Minister Howard made considerable use of task forces chaired by his department, often involving external players. He also engaged people to direct task forces overseen or supported by a reference group of secretaries chaired by his department.

Some secretaries of the Department of PM&C, such as Peter Shergold, have a naturally collaborative style that encourages more frequent and free discussions among secretaries. Others, such as Moore-Wilton or Mike Keating, took a more directive approach to address the government's agenda and their own perspective on it. Whatever the personal style of the Secretary of PM&C, forums of secretaries frequently play a critical role in setting the future policy agenda of the government, and for redirecting policy. Constructive examples in my time that I was involved in as secretary included discussions on housing reforms and the

Council of Australian Governments (COAG) microeconomic reform agenda in the mid-1990s (under Mike Keating), discussions on population ageing and the importance of workforce participation and productivity rather than just outlays on health and welfare (under Moore-Wilton, influenced by Ken Henry from the Treasury) and discussions on Indigenous programs (under Shergold). Less positive examples include policies on asylum seekers and illicit drugs in Moore-Wilton's time, though I must concede that the Howard Government felt well served by the advice received.

As Table 4.5 illustrates, not all of the cases I was personally involved in proved successful in the end—but not for want of extensive involvement by secretaries and other officials.

Table 4.5 The never completed 1995 housing reform agenda

In 1994, I was encouraged by Mike Keating to explore possible reforms to housing assistance programs as part of the then COAG agenda on microeconomic reform and the wider use of competition in the provision of government services.

I initially opened discussions among Housing department CEOs suggesting a new approach to the Commonwealth–State Housing Agreement. I was keen to see the imposition of market rents and the introduction of transparent income-tested rental subsidies to replace the existing formulae for rents (based on income but with open-ended subsidies). I also wanted to explore the possibility of narrowing the differential between social security rental assistance for those not in public housing and the effective subsidies for those in public housing, as an alternative approach to addressing the never-reducing queues for public housing.

The state housing CEOs were mostly sceptical, favouring their traditional approach of publicly owned housing stock with rents set at no more than 25 per cent of household income. The minister, Brian Howe, had also originally supported this approach but recognised the Commonwealth could never afford to provide the capital needed to meet outstanding need, and realised the subsidies for public housing in some locations were unsustainably high, encouraging tenants to stay longer than they needed to and limiting access to others.

Keating and the senior COAG officials supported the use of market rents and more commercial management of the housing stock, but were keen to go further to clarify federal responsibilities for housing. With some support from Victoria and South Australia, we developed more radical options under which the Commonwealth would take full responsibility for rental assistance, including subsidies to public housing tenants, and

---

the states would take full responsibility for managing the stock and policies to promote lower rental housing in the private housing sector. Howe supported this approach as long as it could maintain and extend current subsidies to social security recipients in rental housing in either the public or private sectors.

The benefits were not only greater efficiency in the management of public housing but wider access to low-rent housing, greater equity in housing assistance, more choice and the potential to break-up public housing estates, which in many places had become centres of crime and social disadvantage, limiting opportunities for escaping poverty. There would also be better accountability through clearer division of federal responsibilities.

Keating engaged the Treasury and Finance departments in the process, encouraging them to help address the necessary transfers in funds between the Commonwealth and the states arising from the states receiving market rents and the Commonwealth taking full responsibility for rental assistance.

Housing ministers accepted the proposals in principle and cabinet also agreed. COAG endorsed the proposals in November 1995 and Prime Minister Keating announced the reforms in December 1995 in the 'Community and Nation' policy statement.

Sadly, for political reasons I do not understand, the Howard Government dropped the proposals in mid-1996. The problems of public housing estates, queues for public housing and inadequate rental assistance for many social security recipients remain.

Changes in the role over time

Associated with the Public Service and financial management reforms of the 1980s and 1990s there was some shift in emphasis towards secretaries' responsibilities to their own ministers and to managing their departments. In part, this was a conscious move to reduce cabinet's workload and to rely more heavily on portfolio ministers to prioritise within broader budgetary allocations.

This shift has been limited, however, for several reasons. As argued in the MAC report *Connected Government*, there is increasing demand for cross-agency responses to social and economic concerns, for the government to marshal all the resources at its disposal to find the most effective solutions and for the community to have access to seamless services. As mentioned earlier, the pervasiveness of media coverage has also led to the political requirement for closer control of the policy agenda and of communications.

With the introduction of performance pay and increased use of short-term 'contracts', the balance also shifted during the past decade back towards the collective responsibility of secretaries. The collective responsibility of secretaries is made most clear by the Prime Minister's role in their appointments and their performance assessment. The fact that the Secretary of the Department of PM&C is the key adviser in both these respects adds considerable weight to secretaries' understanding that their legal responsibility to their ministers is balanced by real responsibilities to the Prime Minister and the secretary of his department.

Under successive Australian governments, cabinet and its committees have continued to provide the main processes for coordination, informed decision making and priority setting. The Prime Minister's Office has been strengthened progressively, but unlike in the United Kingdom and Canada, it has mostly complemented rather than offset the role of cabinet. The Expenditure Review Committee (ERC) in particular is the engine room for most of the detailed reviews of policy and resource allocation and for almost all, if not all, secretaries it is the most important mechanism for their interaction with the centre of government.

There have been some changes in the way ministers are collectively advised on cross-portfolio matters. The traditional interdepartmental committee, with each department represented by a senior officer forcefully presenting his or her agency's views based on its functional responsibilities, is now in abeyance and there is more emphasis on time-limited task forces and reviews charged with identifying preferred solutions to particular problems. The task force might involve officers from different agencies but they are not there as representatives but rather as experts helping to find a common solution. Such task forces might involve outside players and might even be chaired by them (for example, the former Prime Minister's task forces on welfare reform and on drugs). They might have a reference group of secretaries whose role includes directing the work of the task force and/or testing its proposals from the perspectives of the different portfolios. Where there is no reference group, secretaries will look to other avenues to influence the task force and to advise on its proposals. Task force reports might go to cabinet or a ministerial committee via joint cabinet submissions from relevant ministers, via cabinet memorandums prepared by the reference groups of secretaries or directly without a formal filtering process.

Another more recent development is to focus on implementation as well as policy development. This began after I moved to the APS Commission so I had little direct experience with the new arrangements. These include the Implementation Unit in the Department of PM&C, aimed primarily at ensuring implementation issues are addressed up front in cabinet submissions with a careful assessment of risks and their management. The unit also oversees a 'traffic-light' monitoring of implementation, drawing to ministers' attention where implementation is not in line with plans and objectives.

Issues

Balancing collective and individual responsibilities is not always easy. Where a minister has firm views that conflict with the views of the senior ministers and/or the central agencies, the secretary can be in a difficult position. The role in these circumstances is still to give the minister all the necessary support and advice, but also to facilitate informed debate in the appropriate ministerial forum. That might involve informing the secretaries of the other agencies of the minister's views and ensuring there is an opportunity for political debate. In doing this, care needs to be taken to ensure the minister does not feel the secretary is undermining the minister's position (particularly when the secretary has advised against the minister's position).

Table 4.6 Michael Wooldridge and control of the health agenda

Michael Wooldridge completed a thesis on the Fraser Government's initiatives on health financing as part of a master's degree. It convinced him of the need for the health minister and department to have control of the health policy agenda and not to allow the central agencies, with only a theoretical approach and limited practical understanding of the sector, to take the initiative.

While at times this led to some tensions, with the departments of PM&C and Finance in particular, for the most part it served the government well. Wooldridge as a member of the ERC felt obliged to ensure his proposals were financially and economically responsible, and we developed a series of budget packages that, while not always publicly popular, were effective, reduced outlays growth and addressed longer-term concerns. These included changes to aged care, the Medicare Benefits Schedule (MBS), primary care, the Pharmaceutical Benefits Scheme (PBS) and the introduction of lifetime community rating for private health insurance.

Wooldridge had Prime Minister Howard's full confidence in these issues for most of the time and in working with the sometimes difficult medical profession. Where he and the department were less successful in retaining the confidence of the central ministers and departments (particularly PM&C) was in public health policy (for example, drugs), Indigenous health (where the minister and department felt strongly that sustained increases in funding were required) and in the relationship between private health insurance and Medicare (it was widely known within the government that the department had not supported the 30 per cent rebate initiative at the time, despite the minister's involvement).

> There were also sharp tensions at times over the negotiation of the 1998 Australian Health Care Agreements, particularly with the Department of PM&C and the PMO (see Chapter 8).

As mentioned, the Prime Minister appoints secretaries after a report from the Secretary of the Department of PM&C. They are acutely aware of the Prime Minister's priorities and expectations even while they are formally responsible to their own ministers. I have written previously of the challenge in balancing these pressures; Brian Howe more than once complaining that he felt I was more concerned about the views of the then PM&C Secretary, Michael Keating, than I was about his (Howe's) views. Mostly, however, Howe was conscious that I, as well as he, had Prime Minister Keating's confidence (from my earlier time in the Finance department and advising the ERC), and that this was helpful to him. For the most part, I think I also had Prime Minister Howard's confidence, but my more rocky relationship with Max Moore-Wilton presented challenges.

A more subtle issue is how secretaries handle the demand for collaboration when there are serious differences of perspective that should be addressed. There is a risk of 'group think' in collaborative processes, just as there is a risk of obstruction and delay in the traditional Interdepartmental Committee (IDC) process. For this reason, I have always favoured the task force approach combined with a reference group of relevant secretaries (or their representatives). Secretaries can find it difficult to ensure different perspectives are fully appreciated where there is no such reference group. It might be too late to advise a minister of concerns about a task force's recommendations after it has reported, particularly if the task force has officials and external people involved. By then, the recommendations might have a political momentum that, if halted, would cause significant damage.

Table 4.7 Collective responsibility or centralisation of power

One of Brian Howe's comments when we discussed a draft of this monograph was whether the increasing power of the Department of PM&C was not so much an emphasis on 'collective responsibility' as the centralisation of political and public service power. He cited the instance, when he was Deputy Prime Minister, of Robert Tickner (the then Minister for Aboriginal Affairs) being excluded from the then government's deliberations of the Mabo High Court case on Indigenous land rights; he felt that the Prime Minister and his department took over the issue completely, rather than just ensuring collective responsibility.

There certainly is a risk that 'whole-of-government' processes do not simply facilitate constructive collaboration and coordination, but involve coopting public servants to serve the interests of the Prime Minister (or other central ministers) at the expense of the interests of line ministers and the groups and communities their policies and programs are designed to support.

For these reasons, it is essential for secretaries to keep their ministers closely informed about cross-portfolio activities and deliberations. There were occasions in my experience when central agencies, at the apparent behest of their ministers, attempted to constrain ministerial discussion of significant policy matters on the pretext of overriding financial imperatives. The Department of Finance at one stage even promoted a culture among its staff of 'winning' debates over resources and policies, rather than ensuring informed discussion among ministers to allow them to exercise collective responsibility properly.

My own approach in such circumstances was not just to keep the minister informed as best I could, but never to accept arguments that our concerns were not relevant because some more important issue was at stake that I was not authorised to debate.

The problem is not a new one, though it has almost certainly become more acute in recent decades. I learned my approach from very early days in my career not to be bullied by the Treasury in the 1970s over family allowances and tax expenditures, or in the 1980s over superannuation and tax reform, nor by all three central agencies in the 1990s and 2000s over Better Cities funding, Indigenous health and hospitals funding.

A related issue is the appropriate role for ministerial staff (for example, from the Prime Minister's Office) in task forces and reference groups. Their involvement can certainly facilitate clear understanding of the Prime Minister's wishes and concerns and help to give focus to the work of the task force. On the other hand, they can inhibit discussion of sensitive issues by secretaries (or the task force) that could be interpreted by ministerial staff as obstructing the work the government has requested. I felt this was the case in the Prime Minister's task force on drugs and, to a lesser extent (as I could personally resist the pressure), in the reference group of secretaries for the task force I chaired on health services delivery in 2005.

Lessons in supporting the Prime Minister and whole of government

The following points are among the lessons from my own experience in working across portfolios and with the Prime Minister and cabinet:

- To avoid misunderstandings about lines of responsibility, do not initiate direct contact with another minister or minister's office (including the PMO), but work through your own minister's office or through the other minister's department. If the Prime Minister or another minister, or his or her office, contacts you directly, quickly inform your own minister or his/her office.
- Informed discussion in cabinet or the ERC is enhanced when secretaries discuss important coordination comments in submissions before they are finalised, and consult on finance 'Greens' (the briefs the Finance department provides to all ERC members on every proposal put to the ERC). Secretary attendance at the ERC is also most often an aid to informed discussion, but ministers should be discouraged from taking in multiple officials or advisers (this only causes other ministers to have less confidence in the minister's capacity).
- Secretary discussion with the cabinet note-taker rarely goes astray after a complex discussion. It can help to avoid a decision being circulated that fails to reflect the subtlety of the issues involved and the difficulty of having such a decision corrected.
- Time-limited task forces are a particularly effective mechanism for whole-of-government action, particularly if there is also a reference group to facilitate discussion of portfolio views as well as (independent) task force views.
- It is usually better if reference groups and task forces do not include ministerial staff, but ministerial staff are invited to attend discussions at particular stages of the task.
- If there is a significant difference of view emerging between the minister and the Prime Minister or other senior ministers and/or the central agencies, ensure the Secretary of the Department of PM&C understands the issues, and keep the minister and his/her office informed of the advice going to the Prime Minister and senior ministers.
- Informal meetings among secretaries are important for cutting through the issues and clarifying remaining differences for ministers to settle. They also help understanding of political factors that are not always reflected in the papers.
- Improved implementation of whole-of-government measures is enhanced not so much by more reporting, but by better assessment of implementation risks when policy decisions are being made and closer consideration of the management of the risks. Light-touch monitoring can then allow selective review and intervention and avoid more widespread second-guessing.

5. The lion's den: respecting and working with the Parliament

The formidable Senators John Faulkner and Robert Ray who led Senate Estimates interrogations during the Howard government years from 1996 (photo by kind permission of the Australian Society for the Study of Labour History)

Elements of the role

Secretaries are responsible through their ministers to the Parliament. They interact directly through:

- appearances before Parliamentary Committees
- occasional constituency activities involving departmental program management
- meetings of government committees
- official functions.

Senate Committee hearings are the main occasions when secretaries interact directly with Parliament and its members. Departments appear before their respective Senate Legislation Committees (still commonly referred to as Senate Estimates Committees) at least twice and usually three times a year: directly after the budget, when the committees are focusing on the Appropriation Bills 1 and 2 for the year ahead; in November, when they have annual reports for the year behind to examine; and often again for the 'Additional Estimates', Appropriation Bills 3 and 4, about February.

Despite the ostensible focus of each of these hearings, by convention, committee members may inquire about any matter relevant to the department's policy and program management responsibilities. I always took the view that, as secretary, I should lead the department's officers in these hearings, unless I was genuinely and unavoidably unavailable, such as overseas for meetings that could not be rescheduled. This reflected my view of my statutory responsibilities and the respect the APS must give to the Parliament. That has not been everyone's practice in the past, though the Rudd Government has now stated its expectation that secretaries appear.

In most cases, a minister formally represents the executive arm of government, but committees are always conscious of the right of Parliament to call witnesses and most questions are directed to officials, ministers intervening when issues of policy (and politics) are raised. For most agencies most of the time, the minister sitting at the table is not the minister directly responsible, but a minister in the Senate representing the minister concerned. This adds to the pressure on the officials to answer questions.

While non-departmental agencies (including the Australian Public Service Commission) might not face lengthy hearings (or might not be called at all), departments are more frequently there for the long haul. In the Department of Health, it was usually two full days each time, from 9am until 11pm.

> **Table 5.1 Lessons for new players**
>
> I remember a conversation with a new Chief Medical Officer as I drove her to her first Senate Estimates meeting when she asked to confirm the meeting was from nine until 11, as she had another appointment at lunchtime. I carefully explained, to her horror, that it was from nine in the morning until 11 at night, for two days, with the possibility of further hearings after that.

It was not uncommon for the Senate, in addition, to establish inquiries into aspects of departmental management or relevant government policies and to require officers to attend. Depending on the nature of the inquiry, I would usually attend these in person also. Examples included inquiries into magnetic resonance imaging (MRI) and aged care, which were particularly sensitive politically, and where major questions of departmental management were being raised. My attendance was not only because of the sensitivities involved and my respect for the Parliament, but to demonstrate to my staff that I accepted responsibility for the administration of the department.

More technical reviews of new legislation, such as on gene technology, would be handled by the appropriate experts and managers. Similarly, I left to the relevant experts advice provided to ministers when new legislation was being debated in the House or Senate.

The House of Representatives has fewer committees than the Senate and they are usually not on highly partisan issues, the government being in control of their establishment and terms of reference. Accordingly, any departmental support required is usually of a technical nature not requiring a secretary to attend.

As a consequence, secretaries are generally more familiar with senators than members of the House, other than members who are or were ministers—and vice versa: thus many new ministers who are not senators have had little if any contact with the Public Service and secretaries.

Members of Parliament also interact with officials in their day-to-day work on behalf of their constituents. Such interaction is usually codified through rules developed with the minister and the minister's office. These usually require, at the very least, that the minister's office is kept informed of any such interactions. I usually took close interest in the development of such rules, but rarely in the real interactions that took place.

Table 5.2 Working with politicians: conflicts of interest for politically active public servants

I have an old-fashioned view that the Public Service values of political neutrality and impartiality have precedence over a public servant's right to participate in politics and that this means that senior public servants should not be members of political parties. Others have different views, and there is no prohibition.

The potential for conflict of interest, however, can arise even at levels below the SES.

In the Health department, the regional director in North Queensland was a prominent member of the Labor Party and occasionally the subject of press speculation that she might be a candidate for the Senate. Her official duties required her to interact frequently with local Members of Parliament, all of whom were from Coalition parties. Some complained to the minister, questioning the director's capacity to act in a non-partisan way.

I had no evidence that the director acted other than professionally at all times. I also felt the option of compulsory transfer to Brisbane or Canberra (where she could be placed so as not to be in regular contact with politicians) was a pretty tough option and could be challenged, quite probably successfully.

There was, however, a perception of conflict of interest held sincerely by a number of politicians. I remained uncertain about the right answer here, but chose to pass on through my deputy a clear message to the director to behave with utmost professionalism at all times and to advise the minister's office that any specific complaints be forwarded to me and that the MPs could make contact with more senior staff in the department if they preferred. I did not receive any specific complaints.

On occasion, I met with government backbench MPs personally to discuss important policy or management issues (not constituent matters). This was more common under Labor, which had active caucus committees that ministers wished to have onside. Mostly, a ministerial staffer would accompany me at such meetings. Under the Coalition, I sometimes (though rarely) met influential backbenchers such as Brendan Nelson on a one-to-one basis with the approval of the minister.

Secretaries also come into contact with Members of Parliament at official functions such as state dinners for visiting heads of state and public meetings and seminars. These provide useful opportunities to meet and recognise respective roles;

sometimes they also provide insights (for both parties) about capabilities, interests and attitudes.

Table 5.3 Surprising insights from future ministers

At one state dinner, my wife and I were seated at a table with a prominent shadow minister, who proceeded to lead the conversation in berating the Public Service. I tried to respond diplomatically. It was to no avail. Moreover, I felt we were being treated as 'servants' rather than as fellow guests (and fellow hosts) at the dinner.

This became particularly clear at the end of the evening when the MP asked my wife and me to arrange more red wine; when I explained that the wine service had stopped, she readily accepted my wife's offer of her full glass! It was a useful tip for when the MP later became a senior minister.

Differences

Dealing with House of Representatives committees is generally different from Senate counterparts. The former are not only rare, they are generally far less combative. The atmosphere of Senate Committees also varies somewhat according to whether the government has a majority in the Senate or not. Even when the government is in control, however, opposition members of committees are still allowed considerable latitude in their questioning of officials. In any case, it is not unusual for government members to take an independent stance on issues of departmental management in particular.

The extent and style of interaction also vary with the nature of the agency and its functions. Departments are closer to ministers and weaknesses in departmental management are more easily sheeted home to the minister and government than are weaknesses in management of other agencies. Statutory authorities most commonly (but not always) escape partisan inquiry and both sides of politics treat independent statutory officers either as professional experts able to offer constructive advice or as (objectionable) decision makers who need to explain themselves. For me, it was far easier as Public Service Commissioner than as departmental secretary (see Chapter 12).

On the other hand, many statutory officers and their staff are less experienced in the political environment and opposition senators do at times exploit this to try to embarrass the government. 'Fishing' can prove very effective and one of the roles of the portfolio secretary in Senate Estimates is to intervene subtly in such situations (see further below).

It was also easier in the Department of Housing and Regional Development than in the Department of Health, with the narrower range of responsibilities, fewer portfolio agencies and less involvement in direct service delivery.

Changes over time

The extent of direct interaction with the Parliament has increased over the years as the level of scrutiny of government administration has increased. More open government, increased Australian National Audit Office (ANAO) activity, the role of the Ombudsman and the increasing effectiveness of interest groups have all added to the legislature's capacity to scrutinise and, since the 1970s, much of that scrutiny is via direct interaction with the Public Service, not indirectly through ministers. (In an ironical reversal of normal Westminster practice, in Australia, it more often falls to officials to explain and even defend the minister, than for the minister to defend officials.)

Corresponding with this change has been the increasing investment by the executive arm of government in measures to manage communications and maintain control of the political agenda. Accordingly, the scale of activity to prepare for Senate Estimates has not only increased steadily, there is now more close involvement of ministerial staff on politically sensitive matters. Public servants are keenly aware that their ministers' staff (and at times the ministers themselves and even the Prime Minister) are watching the TV monitors during Senate Estimates hearings, if not sitting at the back of the room.

Technology is also affecting the process. Committee members these days sit with PCs in front of them, allowing their own advisers to prompt and to draw attention to information that might be used to dispute or follow-up answers given in the hearing.

Table 5.4 Responding to new technology in Senate Estimates

When committee members first started to bring laptops to hearings, we had a discussion in the Health department about whether we too should bring our laptops to allow us to refer immediately to data and documents beyond what we held in briefing folders. I decided we should not, as there is sometimes advantage in taking questions on notice in order to allow more careful reflection not only of the facts but of the context. We did, however, have a computer in the officials' room behind the committee room.

What has not changed much, despite all the efforts surrounding program budgeting and outcomes/outputs frameworks, is the focus of Senate Committee scrutiny. It continues to be strongly partisan, with opposition (and minor party) members seeking ammunition to attack ministers and the government, and government members (and ministers at the table) looking to defend their policies and distance the government from any failures of administration. Questions might sometimes relate to the documents the committee is ostensibly reviewing (appropriation bills, portfolio budget statements, annual reports), but more often they concern issues running in the media already or populist matters that can grab media attention. One can be despairing of this, but it is important to recognise that, as a colleague once told me, 'the plural of anecdote is data'. That is, petty failures that embarrass and grab attention might indeed reflect poor management or complacency or arrogance. Of course, they might not.

Part of the problem is the opaqueness of official documents these days. The rules governing portfolio budget papers and annual reports seem to have left most of them almost impossible to read, and the financial tables under the arcane accrual accounting that is now used do not highlight key issues and trends even for specialists, let alone lay readers. I suspect, however, clearer, more readable documents will still not shift committee members' attention from possible scandals to overall performance and program effectiveness.

Issues of accountability

The most demanding issue for secretaries and other senior officials is balancing responsibilities to the minister and the elected government and obligations to the Parliament, to whom ministers are accountable (secretaries are statutorily required to assist ministers to meet their accountability obligations, as mentioned in Chapter 1). There are formal rules for public servants appearing before committees and supporting guidance from the APS Commission, which coordinates some excellent training courses for senior public servants assisted by the parliamentary departments and the Department of the Prime Minister and Cabinet.

The rules relate to being honest and not misleading, while not answering questions relating to policy or policy advice. The issue of balance comes most often in whether to elaborate a strictly accurate answer in order not to mislead, with the risk of revealing through subsequent questions matters embarrassing to the government. For the secretary, this turns on whether and how to intervene to take a question or to cut off an answer, including where the questions are to officers of a portfolio agency that is not strictly within the secretary's responsibilities.

Table 5.5 Rule 1: keeping answers short

To the occasional chagrin of the minister sitting beside me, I did not always stick to the rule of answering only the question asked, even if that rule is generally a good one. At times, I felt respect for the Senate demanded some explanation of the context of an answer, but I usually

---

preferred to give that myself rather than allow a less experienced person to do so.

I can recall on one occasion a minister doodling rather ostentatiously and constantly on a pad beside me as my officers and Health Insurance Commission officers answered questions on Medicare, the doodling being in the form of a schoolchild's 50 lines, each stating something like 'Why don't they just answer the question. Why don't they just answer the question'.

Sometimes getting the balance right is best managed by applying the 'no surprises' rule, warning ministers of the answers that must be given if discussion moves in a particular direction, despite the possible political embarrassment involved.

Table 5.6 Landing them in it: handling unavoidable questions

When Minister Wooldridge was under attack for not correcting a statutory declaration he had tabled in the House of Representatives to defend himself against accusations of leaking confidential budget information on MRI benefits, I was acutely aware we would be questioned on the matter when we appeared before the Senate Estimates Committee. I therefore spoke beforehand to the minister's chief of staff clarifying what I would say in answer to the questions I expected. He was decidedly unhappy about my intentions, but at least he was forewarned and could consider how best to handle the inevitable political fallout. I warned that, while I would refuse to answer any question about the real advice I had given, I would have to answer questions as to whether I had given advice and, if so, when.

Senator John Faulkner was cleverer than even I had anticipated. He tested me about my understanding of the need to correct, at the earliest possible opportunity, any misleading — deliberate or otherwise — information provided by a minister to the Parliament. I could not avoid giving an answer and I acknowledged that we were aware of the guidelines in this area. He then asked the questions I had foreshadowed: had I given advice, when, whether orally or in writing. I answered each question, as indeed I had to, while knowing everyone in the minister's office was watching on their TV monitors. While he also unsuccessfully sought a copy of my advice, he did not really need to. (The full picture was not all bad for the minister, as he had eventually agreed to correct the record, but I was hardly popular at the time.)

An issue I found particularly difficult was the right of Parliament to access market research collected by a department. Such information is inherently politically sensitive, providing guidance to the government about how to manage an issue, while simultaneously revealing the public relations risks that need to be addressed. My approach was to try to apply the FOI principles, but this was not easy to do.

Table 5.7 Parliamentary access to market research

Senate Estimates were continually interested in the market research conducted by the Howard Government into private health insurance.

The market research helped us in particular to develop strategies for introducing the complex Lifetime Cover initiative, including the language to use and the stakeholders to involve (those to whom people most often turned for advice).

I felt there were entirely legitimate reasons for Parliament's interest, given the risk that the research might be used for partisan purposes and/or that it might be exploited to run advertising campaigns of a partisan nature (because of content or scale). Release of the information could, however, equally undermine the program of government support for private health insurance membership and the implementation of the Lifetime Cover initiative, by informing opponents how they might most effectively damage public understanding and support. Accordingly, release would not be in the public interest.

I prepared some guidance for the department on appropriate investment in market research and consulted the minister's office. The guidance focused on the legitimate role of market research if it was focused on program effectiveness or successful implementation of a new initiative and was non-partisan. It also suggested that the research should be made public in due course, but not while this could undermine the program's objectives or the initiative's successful implementation. This clarified the public interest case and could also put a brake on attempts by ministers or their advisers to use market research for partisan purposes.

I tabled the guidance at a Senate Estimates hearing and gained some temporary support. The support fell away during the next few years, however, as the research was still not made public and we continued to argue the risk of undermining the private health insurance program objectives (the minister and his office had ruled out tabling the research at the time anyway).

I was conscious that this understandably left the committee uneasy about the legitimacy of the research. As a result, we prepared summaries of

---

> the research omitting details that could be used to undermine the program but demonstrating that it was being used for legitimate purposes.

Getting the balance right also involves deciding when to be proactive and how. On a few occasions, I decided to make an initial statement to put on the record the context of a matter under investigation and our approach towards dealing with the issue. While this was intended to put the matter in the best light for the government in the circumstances, and to dampen enthusiasm to go for the jugular, it was also intended to acknowledge the concerns of senators and our respect for the point they had raised. I did this during the MRI inquiry in 1999 (the 'scan scam') and the hearings on aged care in 2000 (the 'kerosene baths' case); I also did it when accrual accounting first came in, admitting openly that the financial accounts in our annual report, while fully audited, were very difficult to follow, and stating that all of us were on a learning curve on accrual accounting.

Table 5.8 Treading the line between ministerial and departmental performance

A perennial concern of Senate Estimates Committees is the slowness of responding to committee Questions on Notice. The health portfolio was frequently singled out, with little sympathy for the much higher number of questions we received compared with other portfolios. The problem was not just slowness in the department: it was gaining clearance from ministers. The bulk of the outstanding questions related to aged care.

After a series of hearings in which the department's performance was heavily criticised, I was asked sharply to explain the worsening record and our failure to take the committee's concerns seriously. I decided it was time to defend my staff. I provided data on the numbers of answers to questions that had been drafted by the department and sent to the minister's office, as well as the (much smaller) number of answers cleared and sent to the committee. Committee members' eyes lit up. My relations with the minister hit a low point.

At the next hearing, I was asked for an update of the data and revealed that hold-ups in the minister's office had worsened and that the department itself had provided draft answers to the majority of questions asked. The committee went on strike. It refused to proceed with oral questioning of the department until more answers to the Questions on Notice had been received. During the next hour or two, I was asked for regular updates on the situation. We had more answers cleared more quickly that morning than ever before, or since.

I have seen public servants go too far, advocating rather than basically explaining government policies and being disrespectful or even dishonest in avoiding answers or giving answers that are just too smart. As a secretary, I was always mindful of the influence my own behaviour would have on my staff and portfolio colleagues. In hindsight, I did not always call it right, but just having the issue of balance always in the front of mind is no bad thing.

Lessons

In parliamentary committees, secretaries are on the stage, along with their senior officers. Members can and do grill you, in large part for the sport of catching out a minister. You are in the witness box and everything you say is in *Hansard*, on the record. Parliamentary privilege represents real power.

The main lesson I drew from my experience therefore was the need always to be wary and to be seen to show respect for the Parliament and its members and senators. Apart from anything else, it is salutary to keep in mind that any one of those interrogating you today could be your minister tomorrow. Most show great respect for the Public Service, but even those who do not deserve respect from public servants nevertheless.

Most ministers most of the time are also very respectful of parliamentary processes and, while frustrated at times with public servants giving away more information than they would prefer, or recommending that embarrassing documents be tabled, they do not usually appreciate public servants being cavalier or too clever. Advisers are not always as appreciative of these issues.

At times, it is not possible to avoid embarrassing a minister. Alerting ministers beforehand to this risk is always good practice.

A minor but useful lesson I learned is that *Hansard* does not reveal silences: taking a few moments to check papers or to consult officers behind you might seem at the time to reveal uncertainty or lack of responsiveness, but getting the record right in *Hansard* is of far greater importance. Do not be pressured to answer off the cuff: no-one sees the delay when reading *Hansard*.

6. It's lonely at the top: management of the agency

Elements

This role of a secretary is closest to that of a chief executive in the private sector, but is still quite different given the accountability structures involved. It involves:

- setting the strategic direction of the organisation in line with the minister's policies
- having a top management structure that facilitates effective overall administration with appropriate lines of accountability
- using this structure to monitor program performance and implementation of government decisions, and to help manage risks
- having staffing arrangements (including industrial arrangements) to ensure efficient and effective program delivery and quality policy advice
- fostering a productive culture throughout the organisation that delivers more than the sum of its parts
- ensuring the systems that underpin most of the operations of the department are robust and seamless.

In policy departments in the Commonwealth, secretaries are also the ministers' top policy advisers and have the associated management responsibility of:

- marshalling as well as adding value to policy analysis and advice.

Strategic planning

I always put great store in strategic planning, consciously trying to avoid the dangers of rhetorical and meaningless vision and mission statements by processes of extensive consultation and engagement supported by real evidence and analysis. Good plans require frank discussion of strengths and weaknesses and of the changing environment. I recall, for example, that the most critical issue in 1994 for the new Department of Housing and Regional Development was acknowledgment that the Whitlam Government's Department of Urban and Regional Development (DURD) was widely seen to have been a failure, and we needed to understand the reasons and how we could avoid the mistakes made by DURD.

I would substantially revisit plans after elections or after changes of portfolio minister, with annual reviews of the plans in between. The plans represented an agreement between the minister and me as to *how* we planned to deliver *what* the minister and the government required (as set out in portfolio budget statements and Prime Minister's charter letters, for example). They typically outlined strategies covering structures, systems, staffing, communications and external relationships, all linked to a small number of unifying themes reflecting the government's broad policies.

The plans were not one-off exercises that simply ended up on the shelf, but were reflected in the business plans across the department and in performance agreements, and were reported against including in the annual reports of the department.

The strategic plans were also complemented by more detailed plans on particular critical strategies such as staffing, communications, IT and financial management. We also undertook risk assessments and developed risk-management plans, though these were not as sophisticated as is now common practice in Australian government departments.

Table 6.1 Strategic plan for the Department of Health and Family Services, 1996

Just over two months after the change of government, I initiated an extensive planning process centred on a two and a half day management retreat. The department had had a strategic plan, but it had little influence on corporate behaviour or priorities and just sat on the shelf. I was determined to have one that made a difference.

The main participants in the retreat were the executive and division heads, but the heads of all portfolio agencies were also invited, as were the ministers' chiefs of staff.

The two ministers and the parliamentary secretary spoke on the first evening and the next morning, responding to questions about their priorities and concerns after their initial experience in their positions. A series of stakeholder presentations followed with open discussion after each group of presentations. The four groups of stakeholders were portfolio agencies, other government stakeholders (including central agencies and a state CEO), consumer organisations (Australian Council of Social Service, Australian Council on the Ageing, Australian Council for Rehabilitation of the Disabled, Consumer Health Forum) and professional providers (for example, Australian Medical Association, Australian Private Health Insurance Association (APHIA), aged care, child care). The presenters were asked to identify significant changes in the environment and key issues and concerns for the national department to address.

I also made a presentation based on my first two months in the job, identifying some major options for addressing the new government's

---

priorities, including in particular the choice between a loose federation of programs in a large department with essentially independent portfolio agencies (a 'holding company' model) and a smaller but more integrated policy department with purchaser/provider or other semi-contractual relations with a wider range of portfolio agencies, many operating on a more commercial basis. I focused on not only the new government's commitments to Medicare and so on, but its stated philosophies of more choice, more use of markets and reduced government spending (including big cuts in departmental expenses).

This all provoked substantial and constructive debates during the next day and a half, leading to a draft plan that contained more substantial analysis of the context than was usual, in order to convince the departmental sceptics that this was not just a rhetorical exercise. It also identified some critical success factors and key result areas, with a number of strategies under each and some initial 'targets'. We emphasised information and communication as priorities if we were to support a more patient-oriented health system and we also emphasised the Commonwealth's leadership role and the importance of our relationships with the many bodies and groups involved in health and family services. Despite some resistance, we pressed for the more integrated policy department option and some restructuring of portfolio arrangements.

The draft for comment was circulated within the department and portfolio and was the subject of a follow-up planning day for the whole SES before being finalised.

The approach was unashamedly top-down, designed to ensure ministerial endorsement, but allowing for bottom-up reality checking.

The final document was cleared through the department's senior management committee, endorsed by the two ministers and issued by me as secretary. It had a major impact on portfolio and departmental structures, governance arrangements, IT planning, staffing and culture. One of many initiatives was a major investment in leadership throughout the department and practical support for a learning organisation.

Management structures

Under the *Public Service Act* and the *Financial Management and Accountability Act*, the secretary has direct responsibility for the management of the department. Staff are accountable to the secretary. Management committees were formally only advisory, but I always placed considerable emphasis on them, particularly in larger departments. They help with the management workload, ensure wider ownership of decisions and foster a shared commitment to strategic directions.

The Health Department Executive team in 2002 – Andrew Podger (seated) with David Borthwick, Mary Murnane and Professor Richard Smallwood (photo by kind permission of the Department of Health and Ageing)

Table 6.2 Top management structures

The basic model that I used was a modification of the one Tony Ayers used in the Department of Defence when I was there. It involved the following.

- A small executive of the secretary and deputy secretaries (or equivalent), which handled most senior staffing matters, discussed sensitive issues relating to ministers and external stakeholders and caucused on sensitive management issues coming before the management committee. It would meet informally (with only a brief record of decisions taken) each week over a glass of wine.
- A management committee that endorsed the strategic plan and any associated planning documents, decided on resource allocations across the department, monitored program expenditure and performance and implementation of budget and other initiatives, and reviewed selected policies and programs in detail from time to time. It would meet monthly, with a formal agenda, papers and minutes.

- Subcommittees of the management committee, usually an Information Management Committee and a separate but associated IT Committee, a Human Resources Committee, Finance Committee and Performance Committee. These were chaired by a deputy or a division head, meeting as required, usually monthly or bimonthly, with formal agendas, papers and minutes.
- Monday morning 'prayer meetings' of division heads and deputies for no more than an hour to identify key issues for the coming week. Each division head circulated on the Friday before a short email with dot points listing the issues, allowing the meeting simply to highlight key areas. These emails were copied to state managers to keep them in the loop and were usually passed to the ministers offices also.
- I also had a regular policy forum of the division heads, plus relevant policy staff, to discuss selected policy issues, usually of medium-term rather than immediate interest to the minister. I often attended these, but they were usually chaired by a deputy.

I reviewed the Chief Executive Instructions which underpin the high level management structure every few years, not only clarifying financial rules, delegations and so on for departmental staff (as required by the *Financial Management and Accountability Act*), but ensuring they reflected the APS Values and Code of Conduct and promoted the culture we wished to foster in the department.

The composition of the executive team is critical to making the top structure work. I always looked to a balance of expertise and personal styles. Subject-matter expertise is essential within the executive to ensure credibility with stakeholders, not least the minister. The team must also include strong management skills. Having at least one person with central agency experience also helps. Corporate knowledge and some continuity are also important, particularly in large departments, and I generally chose not to displace incumbents too quickly (if at all). As explained in Chapter 10, I felt it was also important for the service to have a least one deputy who was a strong candidate to be a future secretary.

As a rule, division heads were responsible for big programs and exercised very substantial delegations, and they had broad management responsibility regarding staffing and administrative resources. The management structure above them was intended to ensure cohesion rather than to interfere. Division heads generally reported to deputies, but I encouraged the deputies to act not as super-division heads but as quasi-secretaries (as mentioned earlier, where there were junior ministers, I allocated prime responsibility for supporting them to a deputy). I always preferred fewer rather than more deputies in organisational structures.

Division heads' authority for staffing was subject to the budgets they held for administrative purposes and centrally determined pay and classification arrangements. The latter has become an important element of a secretary's management responsibilities.

Organisational performance management

While I held each division head responsible for the management of their business units and programs, the departmental management committee also regularly reviewed program performance. In the Health department, we put extra effort into this through the department's Performance Management Committee. This committee would meet regularly to discuss particular programs, focusing on the performance indicators and targets for each program in the portfolio budget statement and reviewing the management of risks against risk plans. The committee might also suggest more formal evaluations from time to time.

This built a corporate ownership of the programs we were managing, allowing the interactions between programs to be regularly reviewed and some cross-program learning to be applied.

The committee also monitored the implementation of key initiatives including major budget measures. This required a project management approach and I frequently established a formal project team to manage some of the more complex initiatives (such as the reforms to private health insurance). The committee also used Gantt charts to monitor progress of all the key initiatives, ensuring I was kept informed of significant problems and could advise the minister accordingly. This was the beginning of what has since become a more sophisticated whole-of-government approach to improving and monitoring the implementation of government decisions.

I encouraged the use of quantitative measures of program and project performance but was always mindful of their limitations and the need for a broader appreciation of how well a program or project was running.

Staffing

Making senior appointments is perhaps the most important element of a secretary's management responsibilities and one that takes considerable time and effort. Selection of SES officers is subject to certification by the Public Service Commissioner, but agency heads take the decisions and run the process. I always chaired selection committees for deputy-level appointments and took close interest in all SES appointments and movements, which were always discussed by the executive. I also monitored appointments and movements at EL2 level, regularly updating information about high flyers and pursuing strategies for their training and development, including through transfers and placements on project teams to broaden their experience.

Having credibility with key stakeholders is also essential to the department's effectiveness, requiring careful balancing of generalist and specialist skills at even the most senior levels. Seconding Professor Judith Whitworth, a world-renowned medical researcher, as Chief Medical Officer in 1997 literally transformed the Health department's relationship with the medical profession, complementing our already strong capacity in public health. When she left, I appointed in her place Professor Richard Smallwood, former President of the Royal Australian College of Physicians and Chair of the National Health and Medical Research Council (NHMRC). In the Housing department, having a small number of city planners, a top team of housing policy analysts and a senior officer with a strong industry background ensured credibility with the states and the housing industry.

I put a lot of effort into the performance assessment system in each agency I managed. The broader process of performance management described earlier closely guided individual performance. Individual performance agreements were linked to program (and project) performance as well as to the strategic plan priorities concerning management of staff, building team capabilities, fostering external relationships and upholding values through personal behaviour.

Assessment against these agreements was also subject to a strict quality-assurance system to make performance assessment obligatory and to try to maintain consistency. The system involved regular direct feedback during the year and the provision of draft ratings by supervisors to their supervisors at the end of the year before final decisions were taken. The supervisors' supervisor would then meet with the supervisors together to gain endorsement that the proposed assessments were consistent.

Table 6.3 The 'manager-once-removed'

The role of supervisors' supervisors, or 'managers-once-removed', is essential not only for quality assurance and consistency of performance appraisal by supervisors, but for mentoring, career planning and succession management.

Supervisors are in the best position to answer staff questions on 'what's my job' and 'how am I going'.

The manager-once-removed is far better able to advise staff on 'what's my future', taking into account past experience as well as current performance, and identifying potential roles and appropriate longer-term development opportunities.

Despite much criticism, I also used a very broad template to guide the performance-appraisal process, allowing departures from the template where a branch or division had clearly performed exceptionally (or badly). I also experimented with upward appraisal, which worked successfully if not linked to the end-of-year assessment but focused on personal development and improvements in team performance.

Performance appraisal formed just one of the elements aimed at enhancing the organisation's capability (Table 6.4).

Table 6.4 Strengthening organisational capability

Over time, I tried to build organisational capability through a series of linked people-management processes.

These processes included:

- performance appraisal
- individual development plans
- statements of required skills and knowledge for each business or team
- training and development plans
- succession management plans
- recruitment and retention strategies.

It was not possible in practice to adopt this framework all in one go: it took several years to introduce.

As each process was introduced and then matured, it would influence the other processes and build an integrated framework helping senior managers (and me) to focus on and improve the capability of our business.

This integrated framework had some important impacts, including a firm shift in training and development to include 'technical' skills related to the administration of programs and the relevant legislation (as well as generic administrative skills such as writing, supervision and leadership), a closer study of turnover and mobility and a more structured approach to recruitment at base levels and laterally.

I could not, as secretary, devote sufficient personal time and energy to drive this agenda myself. I relied heavily on having a head of corporate services and head of personnel who understood my agenda and had the enthusiasm to follow it through. In the Health department, Neville Tomkins and Andrew Wood played these roles successfully for several years.

Every two or three years, the department would enter into negotiations for a new enterprise agreement encompassing some pay increase and/or conditions enhancements combined with productivity measures. I generally negotiated directly with staff as well as with unions, preferring the final agreement to be signed off by the staff (rather than just the unions). The process could be time consuming for me as well as for the senior managers most responsible for human resources as I always attempted to link the agreements not only to our budgetary position but to our strategic directions, which sometimes included industrially sensitive measures such as more robust performance management.

In line with the Howard Government's industrial relations policies, secretaries introduced individual Australian workplace agreements (AWAs) for their SES and most EL staff. Later, there was strong encouragement to widen the use of AWAs to all staff. My approach was to limit AWAs to senior staff only (with a small number of exceptions) and then to use a standard format within which the staff concerned could negotiate personal provisions such as the real pay (within the publicly known bands) and conditions. The standard format was part of an explicit remuneration strategy we developed and circulated, to ensure all staff could be confident of the integrity of our approach and that we were abiding strictly by the APS value of merit-based employment. As secretary, I was always involved directly in negotiations with my most senior staff.

Culture

Fostering a productive culture involves more than setting strategic directions and establishing an effective management structure—essential as these are. Leadership and values are important, even if they have become somewhat 'faddish' terms. A key instrument I used was a common program of leadership development across all middle and senior managers tied to our particular business (health or housing or administrative services). I inherited the customer-focused training program used so effectively by Noel Tanzer in the Department of Administrative Services in the early 1990s to help turn corporate government services into efficient and effective commercial businesses. I used Peter Senge's 'learning organisation' as the core theme in the departments of Housing and Health, those two organisations relying heavily on research and expertise for 'evidence-based' policy and management, and also on external stakeholders with very different cultures to bridge. I was also looking to build a more flexible and agile organisation, better able to manage change and handle uncertainty.

I personally attended at least one session of each of these many courses—Tony Ayers used to call such sessions 'fireside chats'—to clarify to staff my own views on the organisation's strategic direction and to demonstrate my commitment to a more open culture that promoted initiative as well as collaboration. These also reinforced my approach towards public service professionalism and offered opportunities for participants to examine my personal style and objectives. (The almost universal question in 1996 and 1997 concerned my tenure in the Health department: I could assure them only that my own desire was to stay for at least five years but that proved a sufficient commitment for most to give their full support for the directions I was pursuing.)

The purpose of the leadership development program, and related activities, was to gain alignment across a large organisation based on genuine commitment and enthusiasm rather than mere compliance. The key to this was to gain the support of the middle managers—those whom most staff considered to be their team leaders and who more senior managers relied on to get things done. I had become increasingly aware over my career of the importance of teamwork, particularly by middle managers, and the role of team leaders in setting the example for their staff. I was fortunate to participate in a series of remarkable teams—the Income Security Review in the Department of the Prime Minister and Cabinet, the Development Division in the Department of Social Security, the Finance department—and learned that their success was only partly due to the calibre of the individual team members. As important, if not more so, was the example set by the team leaders and the environment that allowed them to take the initiative and to accept personal responsibility.

Complementing the leadership development program in the Health department was an ethics awareness program for all staff, which continued for all new staff (see Chapter 10 and Table 10.1).

Another important tool in fostering a productive culture is the celebration of success and showing pride in history. I was pleasantly surprised by the level of interest and support in the Housing department's celebration of 50 years of the Commonwealth–State Housing Agreements and in the Health department's celebrations of its eightieth birthday in the centenary year of the Commonwealth. The book we commissioned that year from author Francesca Beddie, 'Putting Life into Years': The Commonwealth's role in Australia's health since 1901, in which I took very close interest, was widely commended within and beyond the department.

Awards are simultaneously perceived cynically by staff from a distance and hugely appreciated by those getting them and those near to those getting them—as long as the peers believe they are deserved. I put considerable effort into having some awards for successful teams and individuals, recognising the risks if our judgments were astray.

Enhancing and sustaining capability involve each of the elements mentioned previously but also investments in staff recruitment and training, management and IT systems, and external relationships. As outlined in Table 6.4, I called for statements of required skills and knowledge from each area of the department as a key building block for identifying gaps or potential gaps and strategies for filling them via recruitment or staff development, including staff rotations. These statements provided a more balanced perspective on what was required than had previously come from human resource areas on their own and strengthened the professional culture we were aiming to build.

Systems

We invested heavily in IT, particularly in the Health department. Our longer-term vision was a nationwide system of electronic health records to support integrated health care, but most of our investments were in systems for internal administration and management of programs. Our success was mixed. I believe health managed better than nearly any other agency the government's policy on IT outsourcing, employing a carefully designed project management approach that focused on the business requirements of the department and the then Health Insurance Commission. Less successful was the introduction of a new administrative system in 1998, where our ambitions for improved records management and electronic administration of personnel decision making such as leave went beyond our investment in consultation and staff training. I learned the sad lesson that if management gets the basics such as IT support wrong, it loses credibility among staff for everything it does (this was revealed in our first comprehensive staff survey shortly after this IT failure).

Managing policy advice

Policy advising is part and parcel of supporting the minister (Chapter 3) and occupied a great deal of my time. Management of the policy advising process is, however, a key management task as well. The management structure I generally had in place entailed a central or strategic policy unit and policy capacity within each of the program divisions. The balance was always an issue.

Quality assurance was provided first through the hierarchy, with minutes to the minister required to be signed by SES officers and copied up the line, and deputy secretaries (if not the secretary) always engaged in more substantial policy discussions; the originating author, usually a non-SES expert, was identified as the contact officer. Second, we used cross-departmental processes such as the policy forum and the role of the central policy unit (which, for example, coordinated budget proposals) to ensure wider coordination and to foster internal debate. Failure to consult across affected areas of the department was treated firmly. Policy advising capacity was also enhanced by longer-term analysis, particularly within the central unit, but also through external linkages such as with the Australian Institute of Health and Welfare (AIHW) and the National Health and Medical Research Council (NHMRC) (in the Health portfolio) or the Australian Housing and Urban Research Institute (AHURI) (in the Housing portfolio).

Differences

The main difference between the agencies I led related to their size. Smaller agencies such as the APS Commission and the Department of Housing did not require elaborate structures for control or to ensure collaboration as did larger agencies. The fundamentals of management, however, were the same and the issues very similar. The people-management issues were somewhat more complicated in agencies with different internal cultures to manage (which was true of housing as well as health), but in any organisation they require considerable effort by the agency head personally.

Agencies also have different cultures and it is sometimes important to shift the culture (Table 6.5).

Table 6.5 Enthusiasm, scepticism and cynicism

Balancing enthusiasm, scepticism and cynicism was a common challenge in each agency I led; however, the starting point differed each time.

I found the Department of Health in 1996 to be a rather cynical organisation, too quick to find fault elsewhere and to question motives. The uncertainty created by the change of government certainly added to unease, but did not explain the lack of trust within the organisation and with many external stakeholders. One of the themes of the leadership development strategy was to counter this cynicism through better understanding of the roles and perspectives of different groups within the department and across the health and family services system, while confirming the importance of scepticism (as fundamental to professional advising and to scientific discovery). I also encouraged enthusiasm for departmental policies and processes where these had been carefully developed and well considered within the organisation.

On the other hand, I found the Australian Public Service Commission in 2002 to be an enthusiastic little organisation, eager to embrace new ideas, particularly on management. It had pockets of cynicism, but its main weakness was its lack of scepticism about the latest management fads and fashions. One of the themes I pursued as Public Service Commissioner was to 'hardwire' the commission's initiatives in leadership development and values-based management into the realities of public service administration (see Chapter 12).

Different personal styles clearly affect the approaches of agency heads to management. My own style was probably somewhere between a Tony Ayers (keenly interested in management) and an Ian Castles (keenly interested in policy analysis and relying on others to help manage the organisation): recognising from Ayers the vital importance of people management but knowing that I, perhaps not as much as Castles, needed support on the management side to complement my strength in policy analysis. I primarily used the executive and the management committee to support me, rather than delegating management responsibilities to a deputy, which Castles tended to do. My style was, I like to think, more collaborative than some of the more famous mandarins of the past (recent and decades ago), but my personality required some solitude to analyse and reflect on important issues, and then to take personal responsibility for my decisions. I was sometimes criticised for not having enough 'mongrel' in dealing with under-performing staff, but I would prefer to err on that side than the opposite: in any case, positive reinforcement is usually more effective than negative feedback.

Changes over the years

The importance of an agency head's management responsibilities increased substantially during the 1980s and 1990s with the new public management reforms. These included the devolution of many financial and human resources controls to agencies combined with increased accountability of agencies and their heads for results. The changes were reflected in the new legislation of the late 1990s governing agency responsibilities for financial and human resource management (the *Financial Management and Accountability Act 1997* and *Public Service Act 1999*). Associated with these changes were sharply increased emphases on strategic and business planning, performance management and performance reporting and a tougher financial environment through efficiency dividends and other pressures for productivity improvement.

The primary focus of these reforms was initially on financial management, but in the 1990s, people management became an increasingly important part of the agenda with agencies responsible not only for all aspects of staffing numbers and profiles, organisational structures and recruitment, but increasingly for pay and conditions under enterprise bargaining and then under the *Workplace Relations Act* (to which the *Public Service Act 1999* specifically referred). That act reinforced the Howard Government's policy of industrial relations flexibility, including through individual AWAs. While the Rudd Government has since barred AWAs for the Public Service, there remain considerable variations from agency to agency regarding pay and classification (and conditions) and, within agencies, regarding individual levels of remuneration within pay classifications. Managing industrial relations issues became a significant responsibility for agencies and their heads from the early 1990s, whereas previously these were mostly handled centrally.

Apart from these industrial relations responsibilities, the increased focus on people management encompassed such initiatives as performance management, leadership development, values-based management and workforce planning.

The APS Commission and the Management Advisory Committee fostered many of these throughout the APS, but the detailed work was left to agencies and their heads.

Another important shift in the past two decades has been towards greater use of project management rather than (continuing) program management. The move to more rapid change and to working across boundaries has required managers to be more agile and flexible, relying less on continuing structures and more on time-limited project teams and so on to manage new initiatives or particular challenges and crises.

Not independent of this has been the need for more expert management of communications. This management shift rivals the financial management reforms of the 1980s as the biggest shift in my time. It covers managing communications with internal and external audiences and is now an essential part of managing agencies, implementing initiatives and managing programs (see Chapter 9).

Devolution and other issues

There have been many benefits from devolution, particularly in allowing more emphasis on achieving each agency's business objectives. They were, however, somewhat oversold, in my view, particularly in industrial relations.

Devolution at its height: Andrew Podger launching the Department of Health and Aged Care logo in 1998 (photo by kind permission of the Department of Health and Ageing)

At the time, I accepted the responsibilities and invested heavily in exploiting the flexibility I had to promote the business objectives of the agencies I managed. This included using performance pay to reward individual performance, to allow some pay flexibility for attraction and retention and to engage directly with staff on business improvement and so on. This was all well intentioned, but I now question the value of the overall investment in industrial relations, which was not only of senior management's time but, in the Health department, meant considerable disruption throughout the organisation. I now note that some colleagues gave mainly lip-service to the then government's policies and continued to use essentially traditional industrial relations processes of negotiation exclusively with the unions, and their outcomes were essentially the same as those the rest of us achieved. Some others very enthusiastically adopted the government's policies, sometimes with disastrous effects on their agencies' performance and staff morale.

That said, some flexibility in pay had significant advantages, including the attraction and retention of specialist staff. I signed the first AWA in the APS in 1997 with a new chief medical officer; I could not have recruited her or anyone else of her calibre under the old system.

A broader issue is whether the increased management responsibilities have contributed to a weakening of policy advising. As discussed in Chapter 3, I suspect it has to some extent. I sadly doubt, for example, that the current system would ever appoint an Ian Castles to be a secretary. And I know the time I devoted to management did reduce my capacity to contribute personally to policy development. I do not advocate, however, relieving agency heads of these management responsibilities, which, if handled well, should support strong policy advising capacity within the organisation.

One aspect of this issue is how best to balance the size and role of a central policy unit in a department with the policy responsibilities of the program areas. Linking policy and administration is essential for realistic policy advising. The program areas, however, are inevitably drawn into immediate management problems and shorter-term policy fixes. I tried to address this weakness through policy forums and through strengthening the central policy unit (particularly in the Health department) with some capacity for longer-term policy research. The program areas generally did not welcome the latter moves but, with hindsight, I feel I should have invested even more in the central policy unit. Certainly, one of the key lessons from my experience in the Development Division in the Department of Social Security in the 1970s was the value of a strong, central policy unit with its own research and statistical capacity.

One of the strengths of the reforms of the Hawke/Keating Governments was the more systematic gathering of performance information and evaluation of programs. Cabinet submissions were required to identify research and evaluation evidence in support of policy proposals and to set out how the proposed new policy would be evaluated. In a short-sighted attempt to reduce the size of submissions, the requirement was dropped in the late 1990s, and evaluation was no longer a mandated requirement. While performance reporting continues to contribute to 'evidence-based' policy advising, the loss of internal capacity and systematic evaluation, and the increasing reliance on chosen external consultants, has affected the capacity of departments to offer high-quality policy advice.

Strategic planning, like many other modern management initiatives, can be formulaic, adding little, if any, value. Plans that end up sitting on shelves without influencing resource allocation, priorities and behaviours reinforce cynicism. Critical to making the planning process work are the quality of the information and analysis used in the process, the openness of the discussions involved and the willingness to engage widely within and beyond the organisation. All of these present risks.

Table 6.6 Tea cosies

The retreat to develop the first strategic plan for the Department of Health and Family Services in 1996 (Table 6.1) was one of the most difficult management meetings I ever led.

There was unease about the new government, particularly after the dismissal of a number of secretaries (including the husband of one of my division heads), the culture among senior executives was more akin to that of robber barons than united leadership and there was unease about me as the new secretary.

I engaged one of the best facilitators in Canberra, Lynette Glendinning, to assist me. She has told me often in the years since that it was the toughest assignment she ever faced.

One division head sat in the centre, arms folded and legs outstretched, making it abundantly clear he was there under sufferance. An enormously talented and knowledgeable officer, he was nonetheless closed to new management ideas and determined to protect his particular empire. Our state offices, for example, were merely creatures of history in his strongly stated view and should be strictly limited to working on community services programs and have no role under any circumstances in health programs.

Two other division heads sat to one side, crocheting a tea cosy. The completed cosy, presented to me a week or so later, remains one of my prized memorabilia. I like to think, perhaps fancifully, that its presentation to me was a sign of reconciliation: that its two creators accepted in the end the value of the exercise, recognising my genuine determination for open discussion and wide engagement, leading to a plan that would indeed help to shape the future direction of the organisation.

Performance management is well entrenched in the Australian system of budgeting and reporting, with considerable benefits in the past 25 years in terms of improved focus on effectiveness and efficiency. It is, however, easy to be sucked into unrealistic 'outcomes' approaches with meaningless outcomes statements and limited connections between the program activities and the claimed outcomes. A degree of scepticism is required along with a practical outlook, using a mixture of input controls and output measures, with regular evaluations of impacts; and a broad appreciation of the usefulness of the program or project taking into account the multiple objectives often involved.

Individual performance management remains one of the most vexed issues for any CEO. The most common complaint from staff about their senior managers is the failure to address under-performance; yet, ensuring robust staff appraisal and introducing rewards for performance always face opposition from staff.

Allan Hawke, Secretary of the Defence department (1999–2002), always opposed any formal process of calibration to ensure consistency, suggesting instead the system should focus purely on individuals and how they were improving (or not) each year. My unease about this approach is that it can lead to ignoring poor performance and focusing entirely on pats on the head (or, as Tony Ayers used to complain about such systems, that 'everyone walks on water'). On the other hand, it is also true that most people respond better to acknowledgment of achievements than to the highlighting of their weaknesses.

The other aspect of this issue is the role of performance pay. Despite years of hard work to get a system to work, I now accept that it is just not worth the effort. My support for it was never based on potential incentives to improve performance, but on the discipline it imposed on the process, requiring supervisors to establish performance agreements with all the staff concerned in line with our strategic directions and to provide feedback at least once a year. I have seen too many appraisal systems disappear into the sand as staff and supervisors put off preparing agreements or giving feedback because they think there is more important work to do; I have also seen too many supervisors unwilling to give any critical feedback, particularly when the system does not demand some differentiation in assessments. Despite these risks, I now look back and accept that the disadvantages of performance pay outweighed the advantages. I might have imposed a robust appraisal and feedback system successfully without the pain of the continuing controversy and staff unhappiness with the performance bonuses.

Table 6.7 Making performance assessment work

When I first came into the Health department in 1996, the department had a performance-pay system for the SES (which at that time was mandatory in all agencies). The system was a complete mess and had no credibility with staff. How bad it was became clear to me when I insisted, in the first round under my secretaryship, that division heads advise me of the proposed performance ratings of their branch heads before telling them. Very quickly, I could see there was no consistency from division to division.

I therefore called a meeting of all division heads and, armed with a whiteboard, I asked each in turn to name each of their branch heads and the performance rating they proposed. As each division head finished, I asked the others for any comments. There were none. The lack of any corporate management structure at the time had led the division heads to behave independently, jealously guarding their own territory and not commenting on another's decisions for fear of, in time, losing their own authority to the centre.

As the names and proposed ratings appeared on my whiteboard, however, it was becoming increasingly clear that the standards being applied were hugely different. This could not be ignored when one division head listed his five branch heads and said he proposed that every one be given an 'A' (outstanding) rating. Again, I asked for comment from the others and, initially, there was silence. Then a few said that, while they could not comment on the branch heads from another division, they now wanted to revisit the ratings they had proposed for their own staff. Finally, one said that, while he did not have as much knowledge of the individuals as the relevant division head, he did think from his (quite close) dealings with them, two were not as strong performers as the other three. There were nods around the table. At last, we had the beginnings of a process to get more consistency in the system.

I chose not to press the matter too hard in this first round, but did ask the division head claiming his five branch heads were all outstanding to review his proposed ratings in light of the discussion and come back to me. He did, proposing three 'As' and two 'Bs'. I decided to concur.

Next, I had two angry branch heads contacting me demanding to know how I could have downgraded the rating by the supervisor with whom they worked most closely when I did not personally know of their performance. I met with each of the branch heads, telling them frankly of my determination to get consistency of standards in the appraisal process throughout the department and reassuring them that a 'B' rating was indeed very high against the overall distribution across branch heads.

In time, we established clearer performance agreements that covered program and management responsibilities and targets, with personal development action also identified; and we systematised the processes involving supervisors' supervisors to ensure consistency of standards. Even then, however, I could not say the system was universally supported.

Most importantly, I became increasingly aware in the APS Commission of the research evidence that organisational performance was enhanced, not by performance pay no matter how well designed and managed, but by timely, positive and fair feedback together with clear alignment of individual work requirements with organisational goals and by management effectively removing obstacles to good performance (including getting rid of under-performers). I hasten to add for those critics who have always opposed performance pay, performance assessment and feedback is never an easy or uncontroversial management issue and in some ways removing it from pay decisions makes it harder, not easier.

Another difficult issue in management is building a winning team, moving on the people who do not fit while winning the loyalty and enthusiasm of the others. The division heads I inherited in the Health department were, individually, highly talented and hard working. They knew their areas of responsibility and were generally very good policy advisers. Together, however, they operated as robber barons and it was my job to change that, to build a cohesive team. Sadly, that required encouraging one of the very best to leave. As a colleague told me at the time, you can have a really top rower in your crew, but if he insists on sitting backwards, at some time you have to tip him out. It was not an easy time and I lost some other excellent officers who preferred not to stay and support the changes I was instituting (management change was not the only concern — there was also apprehension about the government's policies towards the public service). A conclusion for me was that good performance required far more than technical expertise, or even good management of a division or branch: it also required collegiality and good corporate behaviour. My own personal behaviour—being as open and honest as possible and listening carefully to everyone before deciding—has also always been essential to building team spirit.

Another issue is the minister's involvement in senior appointments. Secretaries are responsible for all employment decisions in the department and ministers are prohibited under the *Public Service Act* from giving directions on such decisions, which must be based on merit. I took the view, nonetheless, that I should inform the minister before making senior appointments (that is, deputy secretary and, sometimes, division heads), while emphasising the decisions were mine and that the Public Service Commissioner had to certify that the process was properly managed. In the case of deputies, who from time to time act as secretary, I believe there must be a level of 'comfort' about the people appointed.

Table 6.8 Selecting deputies: there's more than one way (for the minister) to skin a cat

In 1994, I was establishing the new Department of Housing and Regional Development and filling the deputy position. In those days, the Public Service Commissioner had final responsibility for SES appointments (subsequently, the role was reduced to certifying the process of appointment). The selection process identified the preferred candidate on merit and I advised the minister that I would be recommending him to the commissioner. The minister, Brian Howe, favoured another candidate and pressed his case with me on a number of occasions. I stood my ground, emphasising the importance of the merit principle and why the preferred candidate was superior, noting nonetheless that his favoured candidate was second on the merit list. I also noted that the final decision was not his, or even mine, but the commissioner's.

At that time, the Minister for Finance determined SES numbers and levels and I had been negotiating with the Secretary of the Finance department, Steve Sedgwick, the SES establishment for the new small department. We were nearing settlement when I told Sedgwick that my minister might be proposing to Beazley something different: a second deputy secretary.

To Sedgwick's displeasure and my bemusement, that is what happened. Beazley understandably deferred to the Deputy Prime Minister, I gained an extra deputy and two people were appointed entirely on merit. And the team worked extremely well together.

Lessons

Michael Keating warned me when I was first appointed a secretary that the old adage, 'it's lonely at the top', was absolutely true. He was right. That is particularly relevant to the secretary's overall management responsibilities. There are aspects of these that cannot be discussed internally at all, including the appointment and performance of deputies. Other aspects can be discussed to a limited extent, but in the end it is your call, including in particular matters going to management style and organisational culture.

Key lessons for me include the following:

- Strategic planning is a vital tool for top management but must be done well. It allows ministers to have confidence that their agenda is being pursued and to influence the way the department does so. The process can also engage middle-level (and even junior) staff as well as senior management, building wider ownership of the strategic directions finally determined. The process can also engage stakeholders, strengthening relationships and mutual understanding and respect.

- Organisational performance management is an essential part of top management and increasingly requires a project management approach to monitor implementation of key initiatives. Some scepticism is needed, however, rather than blind acceptance of the current enthusiasm for outcomes-based management.

- Individual performance management remains a difficult challenge and there is no easy answer. My main lesson is not to run away from it. I no longer advocate performance pay but, in the absence of that, it is important not to drop the ball and let regular and robust performance appraisal slide.

- Structured performance management can enhance personal development and career planning: involving supervisors' supervisors not only helps consistency of appraisal, it opens up dialogue about a person's future (which immediate supervisors might have little interest in) as well as their current job and performance.

- While it is right and proper to inform ministers about proposed senior appointments, particularly deputies, the secretary must not allow the minister to think he or she can decide, and the secretary's decision must be made on merit.

- The personal behaviour of a secretary is critical not only to developing a strong and enthusiastic management team, but to setting the style of the whole department.

- 'Soft' skills of leadership among all managers, most particularly the middle managers, need to be enhanced and encouraged. Having section heads onside is the tipping point of organisational success: they are the ones whom most staff down the line look to as their team leaders and they are the ones senior managers rely on to get things done.

- This needs to be done in a 'hard-nosed' way, avoiding content-free rhetoric. Leadership also needs to be complemented by specific management and technical skills.

- In promoting teamwork, I also appreciated the risk of 'group think', where the pressure for consensus and desire to please peers and more senior staff could discourage real debate.

- Considerable effort needs to be given these days to the design and efficient operation of information and communications systems. These are central to the delivery of programs and the smooth management of the department.

When they go wrong, everything goes wrong, including staff confidence in senior management and staff morale (see also Chapter 9 on communications management).

- The other main lesson I draw from my experience is the importance of allocating time and resources for policy research and development. Pressures from ministers and pressures of program delivery can squeeze capacity for longer-term research and development. Some suggestions for personal approaches to preserve a longer-term perspective and a depth of analysis are set out in Chapter 2. Management options for addressing this danger include retaining a capable central strategy unit, promoting systematic program evaluation measurement, setting aside time for policy forums in the department and drawing on external expertise through close partnerships, including with specialist research or statistical agencies.

7. The art of persuasion: management of the portfolio

Elements of the role

The term 'portfolio secretary' had no legal status and, unlike 'portfolio ministers', departmental secretaries did not in my time have any formal responsibilities over the other agencies in the portfolio. The term is not, however, without clear meaning: the portfolio secretariy is the most senior official in each portfolio and is expected to coordinate various activities across agencies for the portfolio minister and for the government as a whole.

The core elements of this role are:

- to ensure good lines of communication across the portfolio, with the minister(s) and with central agencies
- to participate on relevant boards and committees of agencies
- to advise the minister on structures and appointments and, sometimes, on performance
- to manage formal agreements between the department and particular agencies
- to coordinate portfolio budgets and appearances before parliamentary committees.

Usually, I found the portfolio minister expected a more proactive role than simply acting as a postbox, and also that the agency heads were keen to get better understanding of the broader policy context of their work than a basic information exchange would reveal. Accordingly, I chaired a portfolio agency heads' meeting, usually every quarter, with a formal business agenda but also time for informal discussion. We also generally included on the agenda each time a short presentation by one agency head about that agency's plans and issues. The formal agenda would usually include budget arrangements, industrial relations issues and areas for possible management cooperation; it would also include discussion of current policy issues affecting more than the department, though mostly these would be managed down the line outside these quarterly meetings. The meetings were always strongly supported by the agency heads whose access to ministers was often limited.

I also involved the portfolio agencies directly in the department's strategic planning process, participating in the senior management's retreat and commenting on drafts (see Chapter 6). Agencies usually did the same, involving me or one of my deputies in their own strategic planning processes.

As secretary, I was also often a member of the board of a portfolio agency, such as the AIHW and the Health Insurance Commission (HIC). This entailed attending monthly meetings, although, by mutual agreement, some boards arranged their agendas to allow me to reduce my time at those meetings with another departmental representative acting as an observer for the rest of the meeting.

The department also had responsibility for advising the minister on structural matters affecting portfolio agencies and, in the Health department, this became a major policy issue for several years. The structural agenda included splitting Medibank Private from the rest of the Health Insurance Commission (which continued to have responsibility for Medicare); corporatising Health Services Australia; restructuring the Australia New Zealand Food Authority; and establishing new agencies such as the Aged Care Standards and Accreditation Authority, the General Practice Education and Training Agency and the Australian Radiation Protection and Nuclear Safety Agency (ARPANSA), or new statutory offices such as the Gene Technology Regulator. I established a corporate strategy team in the department to oversee these projects, but many required significant personal involvement to resolve differences and to confirm ministerial views.

Table 7.1 Splitting the Health Insurance Commission

The Health Insurance Commission (HIC) had responsibility for Medibank Private, a private health insurance fund competing with others, and key elements of Medicare, the universal government health insurance scheme. I was acutely aware of the conflicts of interest in this dual role and the lack of transparency in the operations of Medibank Private, which made it impossible to deny criticisms of unfair competition. I advised in 1996 that the HIC should be split.

The then CEO opposed my view strongly and there was debate among the board of commissioners, but the minister accepted my advice.

I established a small team in the department to work with a small team in the HIC to plan and execute the split. For the most part, this project management process worked smoothly and a major reform was achieved quietly and efficiently. The support of the then board chairman was a critical factor.

Drawing from the Social Security department's experience in separating Centrelink from the department, I recommended the early appointment of (at least acting) heads of each agency to facilitate a transparent process for dividing resources and staff, with a clear champion for each new agency. The CEO disagreed, highlighting his statutory responsibilities for both proposed agencies until the new legislation was in place and deferring his own decision on which of the new agencies he wished to head.

My preference could not be enforced, so there was no point pressing the matter, but the CEO's very late announcement that he would go with Medibank Private left a legacy of minor problems (relating to the suspicion or reality that resources were not split fairly) that were not resolved for more than a year after the split.

Looking back now, I have no doubt the split helped both sides. Those responsible for Medicare came into their own, gaining much more attention from senior management, working more closely with the department and addressing a range of enhancements to services and improved administration. Those responsible for Medibank Private gained greater flexibility to operate commercially, as they had always wanted to do.

With the establishment of a separate Medibank Private and the commercialisation of Health Services Australia, the department became responsible also for advising the minister on aspects of those businesses' strategic plans and performance.

The ministers also drew on the department for advice on appointments to all the portfolio bodies, which I usually provided personally after the relevant search processes. That advice was by no means always accepted but I put considerable effort into ensuring a merit-based process for our own short-listing. For the HIC and Medibank Private boards, we employed a search company to identify possible directors, including the chairs, but our short lists were generally supplemented by names (often, but not always, good ones) supplied through the political process.

On one occasion, I was asked to 'sort out' a problem concerning an agency head in whom ministers had lost confidence. Legally, I had no authority, but I was able to counsel her, help her to identify her own options and assist her with a dignified departure when she agreed it was in her own best interests to move on.

In some cases, the department had formal relationships with agencies. In the case of the AIHW, we developed a partnership agreement under which the department set out the research and data requirements it had for the next few years, in addition to the AIHW's core collections and publications, and the funds it intended to provide to supplement the AIHW's core budget. That agreement followed discussions between me and the AIHW director on the benefits of moving away from ad hoc requests and payments from different areas of the department, to a planned approach that allowed the AIHW to invest in 'ongoing' staff and additional collections. The new approach also gave the AIHW responsibility for some collections previously managed by the department.

In the case of the HIC (now Medicare Australia), we had in my time a purchaser–provider agreement under which we negotiated the funds required by the HIC to deliver MBS and PBS payments and so on. This required careful management of my own conflicts of interest given I was both secretary and an HIC board member. We also developed a memorandum of understanding between the HIC and the department to promote closer cooperation and better information exchange on new policy proposals and program administration and implementation of new measures.

The budget process always involved close interaction between the department and portfolio agencies, as agencies developed proposals for ministerial consideration, the department worked with the minister on priorities within the parameters set by the ERC or senior ministers and the department developed its own policy proposals that often affected portfolio agencies (particularly the HIC), which would have some implementation responsibilities. At several points in this process, as secretary, I would liaise directly with the agency heads concerned. They would all have opportunities to talk directly with ministers, but these were inevitably limited and they relied quite heavily on me and the department appreciating their perspectives and concerns. In my time, they never attended the ERC.

All portfolio agencies were usually on the agenda for Senate Estimates hearings, though some escaped scrutiny frequently as the committee focused on agencies handling more juicy issues. Agencies such as the HIC and ARPANSA were frequently interrogated. As a rule, I would continue to sit with the minister when they appeared and occasionally intervened in the answers to explain background or to try to contain the potential debate.

Differences among agencies and across portfolios

Portfolio arrangements vary considerably with the nature of the portfolio agencies' responsibilities. Government Business Enterprises (GBEs) generally value their independence from the bureaucracy and the portfolio department, often working closely with the Finance department, is involved only in advising the shareholder ministers on ownership issues.

Medibank Private rarely attended my portfolio agency heads' meetings, though the CEO of Health Services Australia (HSA) almost always came.

The more budget-dependent agencies tend to have closer relationships with departments, but that relationship can depend on the personalities of the agency heads and their personal relationship with the minister. Small agencies most often have problems with access to ministers and appreciate a close, constructive relationship with the department.

It was interesting as Public Service Commissioner to see the weak arrangements in the PM&C portfolio for informing or coordinating its agencies. The APS

Commission was in a privileged situation given my attendance at portfolio secretaries' meetings and involvement in the MAC, but many other agencies (such as the Ombudsman and the Official Secretary to the Governor-General) felt very much on the outer. I think there was just one meeting of the agency heads in my three years as the Commissioner. This experience confirmed for me the importance to agencies of portfolio secretaries actively engaging with them, though I can understand that this presents a greater challenge for a secretary of a less-integrated portfolio such as PM&C.

Changes in arrangements

The portfolio approach was very much an outcome of the 1987 changes in departmental organisation, which first involved having several ministers in the one portfolio with the one department. Each department had a portfolio minister in the cabinet, some with junior ministers outside the cabinet. An explicit purpose behind this new arrangement was to streamline cabinet business and to give more responsibility to portfolio ministers and their departments.

In line with this approach, the budget process was aligned more formally with portfolios and ministers were expected to prioritise across their wider responsibilities including across portfolio agencies. Some such processes had always operated, but it became firmer after 1987 and has remained so.

The *Uhrig Report* in 2004 on statutory authorities and statutory office-holders raised the question of the role of portfolio secretaries, at long last leading to formal recognition of their role in such matters as advising on appointments and reviewing performance, while not detracting from the statutory independence of such agencies.

A subsequent change to establish the Human Services portfolio including Centrelink and Medicare Australia does present new challenges for portfolio secretaries while offering opportunities for closer attention to service delivery matters. The challenges go to the relationship between such service providers and their respective policy departments and the relationships in turn with the Human Services department. I am not convinced that such separation of policy from administration will prove sustainable.

Portfolio management issues

The main issue to be managed in these portfolio arrangements is acknowledging the independence of each agency and the legal responsibilities of each agency head, while addressing the need of the minister for assistance with coordination, coherence and oversight. Some agencies have considerable statutory or commercial independence, while others are less independent of the minister to whom they are responsible.

The authority of the portfolio secretary is determined largely by the attitude of the minister: the extent to which the minister turns to the secretary for assistance and advice. Most ministers I have worked with do not consciously deny agency heads access to them, but find it necessary in the management of their time and priorities to limit such meetings. For the most part, the agency heads can just get on with their jobs, happy not to have the minister breathing down their necks, but the limited direct interaction with ministers can lead to the minister and the agency head relying on the department and the departmental secretary as intermediary from time to time.

A related issue concerns when functions should be performed outside the department and the appropriate governance arrangements for agencies performing such functions. New Zealanders appositely call this issue 'signposting the zoo'. Notwithstanding its limitations, the *Uhrig Report* has helped, in my view, to clarify some of the key issues and options. Before that report, and despite the efforts of my team advising on corporate strategies, there was limited coherence among the array of portfolio agencies in Health. These included statutory bodies, executive agencies and companies, some under the *Financial Management and Accountability Act*, others under the *Commonwealth Authorities and Companies Act*, some under the *Public Service Act* and others with their own employment powers.

Another important issue relates to appointments. For most of my time as secretary, under Labor and Liberal governments, I was not confident of the integrity of the appointments processes. Despite efforts to use formal selection advisory processes and search arrangements, political favouritism was often a dominant factor. Most such appointees were competent, but not the best for the job, and the process left the likelihood of some political trade. Fortunately, the Rudd Government has strengthened the role of portfolio secretaries and the Public Service Commissioner in advising on these appointments and ensuring a more merit-based approach.

Table 7.2 Shareholder value or gift of the government: the appointment of the chair of Health Services Australia

When the chair of the Health Services Australia (HSA) board, Rae Taylor, came up for reappointment, I strongly supported him given the company's successful transition to that point from a bureaucratic business. There was still considerable risk about the company's continuing financial viability and I was concerned that if Taylor left we could also lose the CEO, Vanessa Fanning, who was performing extremely well, and shareholder value could collapse.

> While I eventually convinced the two ministers concerned, it was clear that they viewed the chairman's position not so much as a key to the company's success, but as a prize—a potential gift to a friend of the government. They were certainly not seized with the possible impact on shareholder value if the appointment process was not handled well. For my part, I felt the portfolio—and the public—had been most fortunate in obtaining the services of Taylor, a former secretary and former CEO of Australia Post, whose remuneration was a fraction of what his time was worth; I also knew he did not regard the HSA responsibility as a prize, but as a burden he was willing to continue to bear.

Another issue involved in portfolio management is the handling of conflicts of interest. The *Uhrig Report* recommended that secretaries not be on executive boards of agencies. I am not convinced this is always the best approach, though it might be in most cases.

Table 7.3 Should secretaries be on agency boards?

When the HIC had a board, I was initially not a member and then became one. The chairman was of the view that my membership represented a conflict of interest, though most of the others felt my involvement assisted greatly in ensuring the strategic direction of the HIC was consistent with the government's policies on Medicare. The chairman, with his private sector orientation, was looking to 'increase the return on the HIC's assets' (in systems and staff) by widening the HIC's (essentially government) business; I saw this as merely another set of new policy proposals to extend Medicare benefits that would need ministerial and cabinet agreement. I firmly believed this difference of view was best settled within the board rather than escalated into a damaging conflict requiring the minister (to whom both the board and I were responsible) to intervene. Conflict of interest? Perhaps, but where was it best managed?

A clearer conflict of interest arose when the purchaser–provider arrangement with the department was being negotiated. I absented myself from the relevant board discussions and delegated to a deputy the negotiation responsibilities of the department. Was this adequate management of the conflict? I think so, but the case here is less clear (subsequently, based on Uhrig, the purchaser–provider arrangement itself was dropped—a mistake in my view).

In the Defence department, where I was a deputy secretary, I also observed the different approaches of two companies being privatised: Australian Defence Industries (ADI) and Aerospace Technologies of

---

Australia (ASTA). ADI had a very able board with no departmental members or observers and was extremely anxious to keep the department at arm's length and, as it saw it, to avoid conflict of interest. ASTA's board was probably not as strong and it included a senior departmental officer. ASTA's sale went smoothly with close cooperation, independent assessment contracted by the department, careful coordination with the Department of Finance before cabinet took its final decisions and transfer of the sale itself to the Asset Sales Task Force. ADI's process could not have been more different. Arguments over conflicts of interest continually delayed and escalated issues, forcing the conflicts up into the cabinet room, where it was clear that it was the board along with its CEO, not the Defence Minister (the main buyer of products) or the Finance Minister (the other 'owner' of the company), that was the odd man out.

Sometimes conflicts of interest, such as in the sale of ADI mentioned in Table 7.3, cannot be totally avoided but must be balanced. What is always essential is that they are openly identified.

Lessons

Portfolio management is still a growing responsibility and the arrangements are still evolving.

The portfolio secretary should never have direct powers over the agencies and will always rely heavily on persuasion, reinforced by having the confidence of the minister. Whatever arrangements emerge, it is important to establish processes for regular and open communications.

It is also very helpful to involve portfolio agencies in the department's strategic planning processes. This can clarify relationships and reinforce shared objectives as well as harmonise strategies throughout the portfolio while recognising distinct roles and responsibilities.

For bigger portfolios with many agencies, it is almost certainly worthwhile investing in a unit in the corporate strategy area to have primary responsibility for managing the relationships and undertaking any work on restructuring, reviewing performance and advising on appointments. The unit needs to be led by someone who commands the respect of the agencies and who has expertise in public and private sector governance.

Secretaries and agency heads (and chairs of agency boards) can also usefully cooperate to ensure the processes for appointments to boards and agency head positions are more robust. Together, they can ensure more emphasis on merit in appointments, even if they might not fully constrain political choices.

There will from time to time be conflicts of interest. These need to be acknowledged and processes for managing them agreed. Avoiding such conflicts might usually be the preferred approach, but frequently they just have to be managed: balancing interests is part and parcel of the political process.

8. Juggling the players: working with external stakeholders

Elements

The main groups I worked with directly as a secretary that were external to the Commonwealth were:

- the states and territories
- advisory bodies and interest groups
- academics and international groups (including governments, multinational bodies and networks of experts)
- the media.

The work included formal negotiations and discussions, consultations, shared learning and information exchange. Working with the media is a particularly complex and sensitive matter, which is therefore addressed separately in Chapter 9.

States and territories

Most portfolios these days must engage with the states. For those with continuing financial dealings, such as the departments of Housing and Health, there are periods of intense negotiations as multi-year financial agreements are developed and settled. There is also elaborate machinery for continuing discussion and day-to-day decision making within and beyond the formal agreements, including advisory councils of senior officials (usually heads of departments), which support ministerial councils. Depending on the workload, the advisory councils may have supporting committees and associated forums with wider participation from interest groups and experts.

In the health portfolio, the main funding agreements are the five-year Australian Health Care Agreements (AHCAs) through which the Commonwealth funds about half of the costs of public hospitals on condition that care provided to public patients is free. There is a range of other agreements including on health and community care and population health (Population Health Partnerships). When the Department of Health included family services, we also had the Commonwealth State Disability Agreements and Supported Accommodation Assistance funding through the states.

The Australian Health Ministers Council usually met at least twice a year for a day with the relevant secretaries attending with their ministers, but more frequently when the AHCAs were being developed and negotiated. The Australian Health Ministers Advisory Committee (AHMAC) of heads of departments met more frequently, usually for two days, with an extensive business agenda that might typically cover public health campaigns, safety and quality, the health workforce, new health technology, Indigenous health, health records and information technology as well as financial arrangements. AHMAC has a small full-time secretariat. Occasionally, AHMAC would meet without other officials present to allow the secretaries to discuss more frankly issues and options for reform. Committees under or related to AHMAC worked on workforce issues, quality and safety and population health.

Negotiating the biggest financial agreements with the states requires delicate handling by the departmental secretary. Such large amounts of money end up being major items for Commonwealth and state budgets, engaging the Prime Minister and premiers and the treasurers. They are also potential vehicles for delivering substantial improvements in services to the community, requiring careful consideration of the details by the officials in the line departments. Within each jurisdiction, there is a tension between the line department and the central agencies, the latter suspicious that the line agencies will collaborate across jurisdictions to lock in future funding for their interests at the expense of each jurisdiction's budget flexibility, and the line agencies concerned that they will lose control of the subject matter agenda (for example, health or housing) and see funds diverted to other purposes.

Table 8.1 The 1998–2003 Australian Health Care Agreements

During 1997, health ministers supported by AHMAC met on several occasions to consider the content of the next five-year agreements, particularly the opportunity to progress reform in service delivery (such as coordinated care) as well as the need to address the weaknesses of the then agreements such as the scope for cost shifting, the failure to address declining private health insurance membership and poor reporting arrangements on outputs. The ministers consciously deferred consideration of the money for some time, knowing that as soon as this was on the table the discussion would be quickly taken over by the central ministers and their departments and moved away from health service delivery issues.

The approach developed during 1997 was to move to outputs-based agreements setting firm targets for increasing acute-care episodes in public hospitals. The proposed agreements were also to provide opportunities to review boundary problems such as support for patients being discharged, GP-type services in hospital emergency departments and care of nursing home-type patients, in part to limit cost shifting. This reform agenda was developed through the Australian Health Ministers' Council, with secretaries playing the lead role. Late in 1997, however, it was clear that these constructive discussions could not continue further as it was time to address the money.

Minister Wooldridge put his proposal for the new agreements to cabinet in late 1997. The department, with my close involvement, developed the proposal. We had just had two of the toughest budgets ever in the portfolio and knew we could not expect generous treatment, but it was also evident to the minister and the department that the Commonwealth had to put forward a financial proposal that would encourage the states to pursue the reform agenda we had been developing. The proposal involved an outputs-based agreement with increasing numbers of outputs reflecting not only population and ageing but increasing demand and improving health technology. A hospitals outputs price index was also proposed. Cabinet agreed to Wooldridge's proposed offer after considerable debate and opposition from key central agencies. Looking back now, I am pleased to say that the offer was more generous, and more consistent with a genuine health reform agenda, than either the 1993 or the 2003 agreements. Given the context of the tough budgets we had, we were pleasantly surprised by the minister's success.

The states' reaction did not reflect our optimism, even though privately several of the most senior state directors-general told me they were surprised by the generosity of the offer. The Premier of Victoria, Jeff Kennett, led the charge, claiming a $1.5 billion shortfall a year—a figure that no-one could explain. Wooldridge attempted to split the states by offering any state or territory that signed up by a particular date extra one-off funding plus access to their fair share of any additional money should the Commonwealth later vary its offer. The Liberal Government of the Australian Capital Territory (under Kate Carnell, the former Health Minister) quickly took this up, to the great advantage of the territory, followed much later by Queensland. I handled some of these negotiations personally, but the Queensland one was effectively signed off by the head of the Premier's department and the head of the Department of PM&C, the two health secretaries sitting in to ensure the details were correct and understood.

In the first half of 1998 there were several premiers' conferences at which the healthcare agreements were top of the agenda. Kennett led walkouts on two occasions. In this period, I had many conversations with my state and territory counterparts to gauge the real gap between the offer and what might be acceptable to their governments. My assessment from these was that the gap was less than $300 million a year and probably about $200 million a year, though no specific suggestion was put to me.

After telling the minister, I spoke to Ted Evans, Secretary to the Treasury, before one of the premiers' conferences and he indicated that, in the general context of the revenue-sharing agreements, such an extra amount should be within the bounds of acceptability, and he undertook to raise the possibility. There was another walkout when the Treasurer refused to vary the Commonwealth offer.

I was then contacted again by my Victorian counterpart, Warren McCann, who told me he was acting with the Premier's knowledge: could we meet to test a compromise option. We met over lunch at a restaurant in Manuka and hammered out a position each of us would take back to our principals. We narrowed the difference to between $100 and $200 million a year, after taking into account the generosity of the Commonwealth's Gold Card initiative for veterans. I passed this on to Wooldridge, who was liaising with the Prime Minister and his office, and to the Treasury. The reaction was positive. McCann rang to say the Premier was on side.

Nothing happened for two months other than continued public haranguing. Then the Prime Minister announced an enhanced offer that Kennett and the other premiers accepted. Perhaps it was mere coincidence, as no doubt there had been parallel private political discussions, but the final agreement was in line with the deal brokered by myself and my Victorian counterpart.

I then arranged an urgent meeting of AHMAC at Melbourne Airport to finalise the agreements, pulling together the content developed in 1997 and the financial aspects now settled. I rang Wooldridge before the meeting to say that aspects of the output agreements and reform measures were not yet tied down and asked how tough an approach I should take. He made it clear that no-one would welcome another public spat: politically, the deal was now done. I led the discussion, proposing to the surprise of my colleagues agreements that reflected the basic structure and wording the states had suggested previously, which emphasised cooperation and shared aspirations, but then worked into it all our requirements for output targets and reporting, and an agenda for examining boundary issues that were disrupting good patient care (we called this 'measure and share'). The wording was agreed and the agreements were subsequently signed.

The potential for conflict with central agencies, and misunderstanding between the political and administrative arms, as well as between the Commonwealth and the states, became clear again when the states demanded a review of the indexation factor in 2000. The situation also reminded me of several earlier occasions in my career when Tony Ayers would say: 'You're being logical again,

Andrew.' It was not meant as a compliment, but as a warning that I was being naive about political factors even if I was right about long-term policy directions.

Table 8.2 AHCA indexation: intellectual logic versus the immediate bottom line

The AHCAs provided for a review process in the event a new hospital outputs price index was not developed in time and the states did not accept the Commonwealth's default position. This situation emerged by 2000.

I suggested some names for the independent reviewer, two of them being put to the states by the Commonwealth: the states agreed to Ian Castles, the former Statistician and previously Secretary of Finance. Castles conducted a typically intellectually robust study, noting in the absence of a hospitals output price index that there was nonetheless an economy-wide output index, the consumer price index (CPI). The CPI is in essence an average output price index and, because hospitals like other service industries are likely to have lower productivity than capital-intensive industries, a suitable output price index for hospitals might be CPI *plus* a small factor, say 0.5 per cent.

This was way higher than the Commonwealth's default figure built into the forward estimates at the time (the case for a lower figure was the evident variation in productivity across jurisdictions and the room for a concerted improvement in efficiency). I was in strife, particularly with the PMO: I had put the review mechanism in the agreements (albeit consistently with the cabinet decision taken in late 1997) and I had advised the appointment of Castles, and he had come up with a figure that would cost the Commonwealth hundreds of millions of dollars.

Frankly, I thought Castles' basic analysis was impeccable even if he had ignored the opportunity for a one-off efficiency gain.

I spoke to the Treasury and the Finance department, Treasury agreeing on the intrinsic merit of Castles' argument though questioning the case for the extra 0.5 per cent (the Finance department then, and even now, seems willing to ignore such analysis if it does not suit). I suggested to the minister and the central agencies a way of offsetting the costs by reducing the output targets in recognition of the huge increase in private health insurance membership during the previous year. Apparently, that was not politically acceptable despite the logic and the fact that it would still have the desired financial impact.

Cabinet decided to reject Castles' recommendation and to keep the existing default index, an index that had no logic and was demonstrably

> inadequate; this decision caused a much bigger problem for the states and the whole health system eight years later. The PMO held me to blame for the dispute for the rest of my time in health, while I forever struggled to gain full cooperation among CEOs.
>
> I remain firmly of the view that, for Commonwealth–state relations to work well, there must be clear policy coherence in any financial agreement so as to foster trust and cooperation. Heavy-handedness leaves a legacy of mistrust and blame that CEOs can never overcome.

The role of senior officials vis-a-vis that of ministers and their staff in these sorts of processes is critical. Officials work to ministers' agendas and politicians will always make the decisions. In my experience, however, officials need some space to do the analysis, to identify the benefits and the costs and to provide an evidence-based framework against which political considerations can be taken into account. Not giving them this space, including through forums of CEOs or other Commonwealth–state officials, runs the risk of constraining the analysis and the options and is generally not in the public interest or, indeed, longer-term political interests. Bureaucrats who play politics can cause just as much harm as politicians and their advisers intervening inappropriately, and I saw evidence of that in housing and health, with NSW bureaucrats more often offending than others.

> **Table 8.3 Looking over my shoulder: the role of ministerial staff in CEO meetings**
>
> In 1994, the minister, Brian Howe, insisted for some time that his senior adviser on housing accompany me to the meetings of CEOs as we developed options for the next Commonwealth–state housing agreement and considered more radical reform of housing assistance for low-income Australians (see Chapter 4). It was a mistake. The other CEOs all felt uneasy, wondering if they too should invite their ministers' advisers. They felt inhibited, as the discussions were not removed from direct political involvement.
>
> As I explained to the minister after the arrangement had operated for several months, the inclusion of his adviser raised questions of his trust in me ('looking over my shoulder') and, more importantly, constrained discussions to the potential disadvantage of himself as well as the other ministers.
>
> He finally accepted my advice, perhaps in part because his adviser had witnessed that I was indeed developing a reform agenda that he might

value and ensuring officials across jurisdictions undertook the analysis necessary to allow ministers to take informed decisions.

Advisory bodies and interest groups

I spent considerable time with advisory bodies and interest groups. Building and maintaining such external relationships is a significant responsibility of top management in any organisation and a large part falls on the agency head as a rule.

In the Housing department, we had an advisory board of business and community representatives, which the minister frequently attended, and the Indicative Council, which gave independent technical advice on investment trends in the housing industry; we also had less formal consultative arrangements with welfare organisations providing supported accommodation services and we were in the business of establishing Regional Economic Development (RED) committees throughout the country. As a rule, I attended meetings of the advisory board, chairing them whenever the minister was not present. I also went to early meetings of some of the new RED committees, particularly where there had been sensitivities over representation.

In the Health department, I moved swiftly to engage with a wide range of stakeholders, as explained in Chapter 3, by inviting them to give a series of presentations to senior management when we were developing our first strategic plan. When we set our vision to be 'the leader' of Australia's health system, we were highly conscious that that required gaining strong standing with the many players involved in the system including, in addition to the states, the medical profession, the industries and charitable groups providing services and products and the various consumer groups and organisations. The scale of health is such that it is impossible for ministers and their advisers to manage these relationships on their own: the department requires close, continuing links and the secretary has to take the lead.

A particular priority for me, and the minister, was Indigenous health. In 1995, under the previous government, the department had taken over responsibility for health services in Indigenous communities from the Aboriginal and Torres Strait Islander Commission (ATSIC). It was a controversial decision and it was incumbent on us to demonstrate that the change would enhance service levels and effectiveness. I chaired the advisory committee established by the minister, a trade-off between the committee being seen to be independent and representative, and being closely plugged into the decision-making process. The committee was one of my hardest jobs.

Table 8.4 Indigenous consultations

The first two-day meeting of the Aboriginal and Torres Trait Islander Health Advisory Committee was a struggle. We spent the first day in a frustrating (for me) discussion of protocols and processes. At about five o'clock, I said that we had now got to know each other and settled our processes, but perhaps we could be more 'businesslike' and return to the substantial agenda on the second day.

My comment caused a furore. I was accused of racism and of ignoring 'blackfellas'' way of doing business. Debate on my comment continued for more than an hour the next morning, before we turned to matters directly relevant to health services for Indigenous people.

I accepted I might have spoken presumptuously, but I also knew this was a try-on, a game to test my nerve and patience. It was by no means the last time discussions with the National Aboriginal Community Controlled Health Organisation (NACCHO) and other Indigenous organisations got testy (leading to occasional cessation of grants and withdrawal of agreements), but over subsequent years, I and the department gained considerable respect from most Indigenous organisations for the mix of empathy, patience, toughness and professionalism we tried hard to demonstrate.

There was no doubt in my mind that my direct and continuing involvement was essential and I followed up formal meetings with many visits and informal discussions with community leaders. It was hard work, but inherently satisfying because it was the most important responsibility we had. We made some progress, aware of the evidence that community involvement was critical to improved health, but were frequently overwhelmed by the complexity of the problems and despairing about how to engage and to understand the cultural diversity involved.

The late Puggy Hunter was a key character in those years. A Kimberley man, Hunter had many parts. He was a pragmatist, willing to negotiate across the political divide to get better resources for Indigenous health services, but he had his own battles in the arcane world of Aboriginal politics. Despite being chair of NACCHO, he could not always deliver his side of the bargain with his network, nor could he always get from government what his network demanded. The divide between the old school led by Naomi Meyer, the pioneer of the Redfern Aboriginal Medical Service, who saw the issues primarily through the lens of rights and struggles and protest, and the new school of pragmatists looking for practical gains and willing to negotiate, was and remains wide. The old school is not without its justification, but Indigenous health needs people to work together.

My greatest disappointment was Minister Wooldridge not convincing cabinet to commit to an increasing budget allocation, which I firmly believed was required and could be well spent. He tried hard, and indeed he delivered real increases each year, but his attempts to lock in more substantial increases every year for 10 years received no support from his ministerial colleagues.

Working with external groups often goes beyond consultation. Some interest groups have the capacity to make or break a government initiative and proposed measures have to be negotiated with them. This was particularly true in health, where agreements were continually being negotiated with the AMA and the various colleges such as the pathologists, radiologists and GPs, and the Pharmacy Guild. My role in these was usually not in the negotiations themselves but in some of the early high-level discussions of the possible parameters for negotiations.

Table 8.5 Learning the limits: negotiating the GPs' memorandum of understanding in 1999

The first memorandum of understanding (MOU) with GPs (the Royal College, the Divisions of General Practice and the AMA) was negotiated in 1996, with increases in MBS fees agreed in exchange for restrictions on the growth in numbers of GPs through vocational registration. The agreement came up for renegotiation in 1999.

The department and I advised the minister that he should press hard for firmer conditions on MBS fee increases, including a greater shift towards blended payments (some funds based on patient numbers—'capitation'—rather than just fee-for-service) by introducing more payments for particular purposes such as immunisation, cancer screening, practice support and chronic illness care planning, providing greater incentives for group practices and reducing rewards simply for throughput. I also canvassed the possibility of placing conditions relating to the co-payments charged. The minister was keen to make some progress particularly on improving public health outcomes and chronic illness care, agreeing that this might allow some shift to blended payments and more sensible incentives (rewarding quality and effort) for GPs, but he cautioned that my preferred approach was a bridge too far. I did not agree and told him so. I was wrong.

After cabinet agreement, the minister successfully negotiated his deal with the then AMA President, David Brand, the Royal Australian College of General Practitioners and the Divisions of General Practice. Then there

---

was an election for the AMA Presidency at which Dr Brand was defeated by Dr Kerryn Phelps in a major medico-political brawl over the GPs' MOU. The MOU, which I felt was too soft, was in fact too hard (at least for the AMA at the time).

Relations with the AMA entered a very rocky period, Wooldridge finally and famously making concessions to Phelps at a Sydney restaurant in front of television cameras. I strongly suspect that GPs in fact lost financially out of the compromise, but progress on reform was also slowed.

Table 8.6 Consulting with the private health insurance industry

I met the private health insurers in 1997 to discuss possible directions for reform and put on the table the possibility of changing community rating to an unfunded lifetime approach, as suggested in the recent report by the Productivity Commission (on our advice).

They did not reject this suggestion out of hand, but were keener on increasing the direct support they received from government, arguing that this was justified in recognition of the savings to government as their members relied less on public hospitals. My preferred approach was set aside until after the 1998 election (the minister wisely deciding it could be derailed in the heat of an election given the complexities involved). We met again subsequently to discuss specific possibilities. The details were developed during the next year in close consultation with the industry; the funds were also engaged in the communications strategy in 2000 that was essential to explain what was a highly complex policy initiative.

As it turned out, this initiative was far more effective in reversing the downward spiral in private health insurance membership than any of the previous initiatives involving direct subsidies.

Academics and international networks

An element of this role of a secretary that I was personally very keen about was engaging with academics and international groups and individuals. I always took seriously the idea of us delivering 'world-class' services, requiring us to know the lessons from the past and to know of international developments.

In the Housing department, Minister Howe was also keen on academic linkages and he had a history of establishing reviews that, while very closely tied to his political agenda, drew considerably on academic expertise. When I arrived in housing, he had in place Jenny Macklin's review of urban and regional planning and the portfolio had close links with the Australian Housing and Urban Research Institute (AHURI) and the Centre for Urban Research and Action in Melbourne.

In Health, the National Health and Medical Research Council (NHMRC) ostensibly provided the umbrella for linking with the research community, but its emphasis was on medical research and I struggled for six years to get the council to focus seriously on public health, health services delivery or health economics (despite two review reports, endorsed by the government, giving them extra resources precisely for these purposes). I tended to look elsewhere, attending seminars and conferences of experts from various universities. Professor Stephen Leeder at Sydney University was particularly helpful in the early days, hosting a regular private forum attended mostly by NSW health officials and Sydney University academics, which I participated in whenever I could. Despite time problems, I also tried to keep up with the literature on health financing and economics in particular, and encouraged officers in the department to do likewise.

Our own Occasional Papers series imposed a good discipline on our analysis and required officers to do the necessary research and maintain academic contacts. It also provided a further opportunity for subsequent engagement with academics, who generally responded very favourably to the work. Some of the papers derived from seminars we hosted with selected academics. They also posed some political challenges (see Chapter 9).

Ever since my time in the Social Security department in the early 1980s, I have also drawn on international networks of practitioners and academics. I attended a major Organisation for Economic Cooperation and Development (OECD) conference in 1980 that led to a seminal report, *The Welfare State in Crisis*, and the establishment in 1983 of the OECD's Working Party Number One on social welfare. I was made chair of the working party when in the Finance department and used the opportunity to forge many lasting contacts. In the Health department, I generally left to the Chief Medical Officer the main responsibility for our relationship with the World Health Organisation (WHO), while keeping a personal role in our relationship with the OECD, which offered considerable opportunities for learning about health systems and looking at our own system from an external perspective. One senior officer in the department, Dallas Arriotti, had particularly strong international connections and she helped me on several occasions to develop itineraries for international trips for the minister and myself. She was also successful in getting me involved with a fascinating network called Four Nations (Table 8.7).

Table 8.7 The Four Nations network

This network, led by a small group of individuals with high standing in the fields of health and political science, focused on the health systems of the Netherlands, Germany, Canada and the United States. Participants included academics and practitioners (public servants, politicians, service providers) from each of the four nations and other international experts, including from the OECD, the World Bank and WHO and from the United Kingdom and Ireland.

Three of the countries have universal health systems, three are federations and three have significant private financing: for these reasons, they are relevant to Australia. More importantly, the participants were a veritable who's who of international experts in health systems and public administration.

The format was informal, but supported by documents from the four nations on a particular issue (for example, primary care, hospitals, aged care) and a commissioned commentary from an international expert observer. Because most participants attended regularly, there were opportunities for much deeper learning than through other forums I attended and I liked their philosophy of 'learning about before learning from'.

While I sometimes took another departmental officer with me, I used this network personally to reflect on our health system, to consider whether and how to adapt useful developments elsewhere and to test some of our own ideas. We hosted one meeting of the group in Sydney in 2000. In 2005, well after leaving the Health department, when I was chairing the review of the delivery of health services for the Prime Minister, I renewed my contacts with this network and received some helpful advice—not on what we should do in Australia but more on what questions I should pursue in the review.

These days, departments are increasingly involved in working with developing nations and more widely on trade issues. In the Housing department, Minister Howe was particularly interested in China, Japan and Indonesia and their efforts in urban infrastructure. I followed up his initiatives in Japan, in particular negotiating access for Australian firms to Japanese building markets. In the Health department, I was again involved with China, and the department with Japan, Indonesia and Malaysia.

Four Nations Conference in Germany in 1997 – Andrew Podger with Dr Zipperer, head of the German Health Department (personal photo collection of Andrew Podger)

Table 8.8 Overseas visits have their moments

My trip in 1994 to China, Japan and Indonesia with Brian Howe was memorable for many reasons.

At my instigation, the minister agreed that a prominent businessman, Brian Martin, would accompany us. We were all impressed with the huge housing and urban development under way in China, but the minister seemed surprised when I said I was decidedly unenthusiastic about the prospects for much trade in this area. Martin reinforced my views, noting the huge risks to any private investment in the absence of international contract law and political certainty. There were certainly potential benefits in government-to-government cooperation and helping China learn about such matters as urban planning in a market economy, renewal of historic buildings and precincts and asset management, but Australian private sector involvement in the industry in China was unlikely to go much beyond simple fee-for-service consultancies for some time.

In Beijing, we met with Zhu Rhonggi, one of China's most remarkable leaders at the time and formerly the very progressive Mayor of Shanghai. He discussed frankly the challenges facing China socially and economically, including the expected shift of population from having

80 per cent in rural areas to 60 per cent in the cities within 20 years—that is, a movement of about 500 million people. He spoke about opening up markets, reforming collectives, addressing growing inequity by transferring taxation powers from the provinces to the centre to allow redistribution to poorer provinces and privatisation of roads and utilities. His agenda was like a concertina of our past reforms over 50 years or more and our current reforms.

We also met the Mayor of Beijing, who greeted us wearing a Sydney Olympics tie. When we asked why he thought Beijing had lost to Sydney in the very recent competition, he answered frankly, 'Blue skies, blue sea'.

Among the most memorable of many fascinating experiences was our visit to Tianjin on a Sunday. We met with the Australian Studies Centre at the university before having lunch with city officials at the Buckingham Palace Restaurant in the Astor Hotel in the old 'treaty port' with its colonial architecture. It was an amazing event.

We were welcomed by a small chamber group dressed up in Mozart costumes complete with wigs and powdered faces. For our banquet, we sat at a long table with high-backed chairs and golden goblets. Our host, the deputy mayor, a female engineer, quickly became decidedly drunk. The minister, sitting in an even higher-backed chair than the rest of us (almost a throne), turned to me to ask what he might say. I suggested he take this once-in-a-lifetime opportunity to raise a toast to the Australian republic in Buckingham Palace. He did so with great enthusiasm, and much mirth among the Australian contingent.

Dinner with Chinese Vice President, Zhu Ronggii, in 1994: Renata Howe on his right, and on his left the interpreter, Andrew Podger, Jenny Macklin and Professor David Wilmot (personal photo collection of Andrew Podger)

Table 8.9 Overseas visits also have their downsides

My first trip overseas with Michael Wooldridge was just after the 1996 budget. It was a tough budget with cuts everywhere. The only new spending was an increase in the subsidy for private health insurance premiums. We went to the United Kingdom and North America, having agreed clear lines for those staying behind to respond to all the criticism we anticipated over the cuts.

To limit jetlag, I stayed up for as long as I could on the day we arrived and we then had a full day of meetings and a dinner the next evening. At one o'clock the next morning, I received my first call from Canberra: private health insurance premiums were increasing and the media and opposition were highlighting that this premium increase would fully offset the subsidy increase. What should we say? The government's only good news in the budget had gone sour.

I did my best to discourage the knee-jerk reaction to involve politicians in the setting of premiums, noting the department's statutory role (which I did not much like either) and the benefits of an arm's-length process.

An hour or so later, there was another call. There was now a suggestion of a public inquiry. I advised firmly against that, warning that inquiries should not be established without some clear strategy in mind and the new government could come under attack if there was any public uncertainty about its support for Medicare.

A few hours and several calls later, I decided I had better wake up the minister's adviser, Ken Smith. We went through the issues and he agreed with my advice, and that we should not wake the minister until the morning.

By this time, however, it was evening in Canberra and the press needed answers. The Prime Minister and Treasurer were involved and wanted to speak to Wooldridge. We set a time (about 8am, I think) and woke the minister just after 6am. He agreed with the position we proposed: do not have ministers buy into the premium setting and do not have an inquiry. The telephone call was made and the minister presented his views.

Decisions were then taken in Australia: premiums were to be subject to agreement by a committee of the Prime Minister, the Treasurer and the Health Minister and the Productivity Commission was to conduct an inquiry into private health insurance.

The lesson? Advice from overseas has no authority or influence.

Differences across government

The extent of external engagement activity varies considerably across Commonwealth departments according to their functional responsibilities. For me, it was greatest in the Health department, which Sidney Sax famously described as 'a strife of interests'. Commonwealth–state issues are also most complicated in health, though they also play an important role in many other portfolios these days. Similarly, international connections vary across departments—the Department of Health possibly having more than most.

There are also personal factors involved, with some secretaries preferring to limit their own involvement, and exposure, relying more on ministers and their staff to manage external relationships or, at least, requiring that their engagement with stakeholders is always confidential rather than public. I generally enjoyed this role, believing it made me better aware of the issues and different perspectives and hence better able to advise, and accepting such engagement could not be expected to be off the record (indeed, there were benefits from the discipline and wider interaction that flowed from public engagement). I also placed emphasis on the credibility of my agencies among the stakeholders and saw public interest in the information I was able to provide via public speeches and private consultations. I also enjoyed interacting with academics, finding this personally stimulating. Other secretaries are more reserved and rely more heavily on private and informal interactions rather than public forums. The days of isolation and anonymity, however, are long since gone.

Ministers' preferences also have an impact, some encouraging wider interaction and others being less keen. Brian Howe was particularly keen for his small department to have strong connections in Australia and internationally, including with the academic community. Michael Wooldridge also promoted widening and deepening the department's work with external stakeholders, particularly among health professionals.

Recent changes in the interaction

Curiously, while the management of external relationships has grown steadily in importance across all government agencies, the sensitivities involved have also grown, leading to increasing attempts to manage the process centrally through ministers' offices and the PMO.

The Management Advisory Committee report *Connected Government* sets out some of the reasons for more interaction across and beyond government, including the technological capacity to do so, increasing community expectations and our increasingly informed and educated public. Looking simply at Commonwealth–state relations, there continues to be an almost inexorable increase in the national government's involvement in public policy, whether in service delivery or economic and environmental regulation. So far, the states have not vacated these fields, so the extent of joint involvement has widened. More generally, the increasing number of players on the field, and their increasing professional capacity, requires secretaries to keep up to meet their basic responsibilities of offering disinterested but highly informed advice.

The international agenda is also inexorably increasing, so that almost every department now has its own networks among similar developed nations and very different, developing nations, and relies less heavily on the Department of Foreign Affairs and Trade. Most secretaries travel overseas several times a year, with and without their ministers.

Engagement with academics has moved in both directions. The Hawke/Keating Governments encouraged close connections with academia. Howe reflected this attitude when I was secretary of his department, encouraging us to engage with external centres and academics. The Howard Government seemed less enthusiastic on the whole, though Wooldridge was keen for us to consult public health and medical researchers in particular. The government's unease, not often shared by Wooldridge, was more with consulting health economists known to be critical of private health financing and promoting closer control of doctors (indeed, I was instructed not to consult certain external experts when conducting the review of health services delivery for the Prime Minister in 2005). Nonetheless, a number of departments have strengthened their relationships with universities in recent years, including through contracted research, as they struggle to maintain research capability internally.

Issues arising

An issue in all areas of working with stakeholders is the respective roles of secretaries (and their departments) and ministers (and their offices). The modern world demands that secretaries and their departments engage more widely, but as they do so, political risks arise that need to be managed carefully.

In working with the states, forums of officials are essential for marshalling the information and analysis and clarifying the key issues for political settlement. Not allowing the officials some space to work without direct political involvement (or having political bureaucrats) can undermine the ability for dispassionate analysis and information sharing. Secretaries play a key role in overseeing these processes and in maintaining the confidence of ministers that the process is working in their interests, giving them the opportunity to consider relevant policy options and make well-informed decisions.

Likewise, in dealing with interest groups, ministers understandably need to be confident that departmental contacts are constructive and supportive of the government's agenda and are not likely to exacerbate political difficulties. A risk, if that confidence is lacking, is that ministers see secretaries and their departments as just one source of advice competing with others, where the competition for ideas is managed directly in the office. Vital to informed debate and good decision making is the availability of disinterested public service advice that is well informed of different views and able to provide analysis of them. Smart interest groups will liaise with departmental officers as well as ministerial staff; wise ministers will encourage this and refer proposals from interest groups to departments for analysis and advice. Secretaries are key to getting these processes right.

There can also be a risk in ministers expecting their secretaries to maintain close relationships with stakeholders, particularly those they themselves draw on regularly. Secretaries must also demonstrate to their staff and to the wider public that such relationships do not reflect any partiality. Accordingly, it is important to ensure relations with organisations that are not known supporters of the government are also maintained, notwithstanding the occasional displeasure of ministerial staff. It is also important to resist undue pressure to offer consultancies to those close to the minister without proper process.

Maintaining international connections also raises the issue of containing costs to taxpayers and ensuring value for money. International travel is always seen as a perk by the media, and such criticism is often unfair. I do not know if I always got the balance right, but I generally went overseas with the minister once a year, letting another senior officer accompany him if there were other visits, and I might have had a separate visit each year focusing on my own contacts while attending to some specific business. Sometimes there were other brief visits for specific business purposes.

Lessons

Secretaries these days do have to spend more of their time managing external relationships. Even when they are not directly engaging with external organisations, they must oversee the relationships and ensure there is comfort at the ministerial level about the processes involved, that they support the government's agenda and that the people involved can be trusted.

Managing the relationships requires effort to appreciate different cultures as well as different views and to help staff understand that in complex fields such as health it is not possible simply to direct. Often, success is reliant on influencing key players to cooperate even if they do not fully agree. In this context, the idea of 'leadership' encouraged by the APS Commission does indeed have real meaning and value.

In a similar vein, I learned to take a pragmatic approach to working with the states. Notwithstanding the benefits of clearly defined roles and responsibilities (which I still strongly advocate), there will always be many areas where one level of government wishes to influence another and these areas change from time to time. For these reasons, I thought in terms of 'control, influence, appreciate': try to clarify who controls what, identify and negotiate areas where one jurisdiction wishes to influence another and always appreciate the remaining areas under the others' control, as some understanding of the issues and challenges can be important into the future.

I believe strongly that secretaries benefit from personal involvement in external networks, whether they are networks of academics or international experts or of experienced non-government players. These networks provide rare opportunities to look at the department, or the wider system in which it operates, from an external perspective. Such perspectives quite often lead to significant reassessment of strengths and weaknesses, and where effort needs to be placed in the medium to longer term.

9. Fourth estate or fifth column? Working with the media

Perhaps the most sensitive external group a secretary interacts with is the media. Particularly in the Howard Government years, any direct interaction had to be handled with great care. The relationship between politics and the media has always been critical and, also, essentially symbiotic. The Public Service and particularly departmental secretaries are inevitably affected by this relationship whether or not they have direct, personal contact with journalists. In my experience, one of the greatest changes in public administration during the past 30 years has been the increased importance and sophistication (and sensitivity) of communications management.

Elements of the relationship

The main ways in which departments and secretaries are involved directly or indirectly with the media are:

- the daily routine of monitoring stories, preparing briefs and liaising with the minister's office
- planning for communications to support program management and implementation of new initiatives
- presenting public speeches and publishing papers and reports
- responding to freedom-of-information (FOI) requests
- speaking directly to journalists and commentators.

Aspects of some of these elements have been discussed in Chapter 3 ('Working with ministers') and Chapter 6 ('Managing the department'), but they are of such significance as to warrant attention in their own right.

The daily routine

The daily routine starts with the circulation early each morning of *Media Monitors*—in my day, via stapled photocopies of all that day's newspaper stories relevant to the portfolio and a listing of other relevant media stories from radio, television and magazines (now the material is circulated online). *Media Monitors* are circulated to almost all SES officers as well as the minister and all advisers. The public affairs unit or ministerial support unit in the department organises this and ensures someone has scanned the stories at a very early hour in case of a big, breaking story possibly requiring response for early morning radio. I would normally scan *Monitors* when I arrived in the office about 8.30am. By 9am at the latest, the stories that seem likely to 'get a run' have been identified and agreement reached with the minister's office on whether briefing is required for the minister.

Most days, I would not participate in this directly, although, by scanning *Media Monitors*, I was always ready to do so if I felt it necessary. Our Monday morning 'prayer meetings' of division heads and deputies would also have discussed expected media interest in the portfolio that week when identifying key issues (see Chapter 6), and helped to clarify our priorities.

The importance and urgency of ministerial briefings increased on parliamentary sitting days when Question Time Briefs (QTBs) were required. Division heads normally took responsibility for the quality of these and ensured liaison with the minister's office, but when big stories were running I would often intervene personally, along with the relevant deputy secretary. As mentioned in Chapter 3, in cases such as the 'Scan scam' and 'kerosene baths', we implemented a major project management approach.

The public affairs unit would also keep an eye on the media cycle during the day, as newspaper stories were followed up first by ABC radio and then by talkback radio, and in the evening by popular and in-depth public affairs TV.

In the Department of Health, this routine was a huge task. Stories on health appear in every newspaper every day, often with a page-one headline and usually with a headline on one of the first five pages. Ministers and secretaries must get used to this, accepting the environment without being panicked, but also discerning which stories need high-level attention and how best to respond. The political imperative is to dampen down the bad-news stories and the department's briefing certainly aims to help the minister achieve that. I always felt, however, that it was also important to inform and educate the public on complex matters of policy or management and encouraged the inclusion of background information if not in the brief itself then in an attachment. Mostly, this also reinforced the political objective of dampening down a crisis story.

Proactive communications management

Communications management these days also has a proactive element. Cabinet submissions usually include, as the first attachment, a draft press release indicating how the proposed measure might be presented to the public. This has long been the case, but now there is usually a more sophisticated communications strategy behind the press release and departments maintain a considerable continuing investment in capacity for market and other communications research and communications campaigns.

Table 9.1 Red and blue umbrellas: explaining lifetime cover

The decision to introduce unfunded lifetime community rating to replace the previous community rating regulation of private health insurance presented a considerable challenge for communications: how to explain a complex reform and how to maximise its effectiveness in meeting the government's objectives of increased private health insurance membership and more stable premiums.

Communications considerations had already influenced the detail of the reform, including its simple profile of increasing premiums by age (very broadly reflecting increasing health costs by age). The market research contributed to the strategies for involving pharmacists and GPs extensively, as these were the main groups people said they would turn to for independent advice. The research also contributed to the name 'lifetime cover' as an accurate, simple and positive reflection of the reform.

The communications strategy drew on expert advice from the industry and elsewhere on the time needed to inform the community and allow them to make a considered decision, noting the potential negative impact on those who delayed deciding beyond the deadline set.

It also built on the earlier communications strategy surrounding the private health insurance tax rebate involving red and white striped umbrellas signifying 'cover'. (That strategy included government advertising and complementary advertising by the industry and individual funds, all using the umbrellas.) The new strategy introduced blue and white striped umbrellas.

The scale of government advertising was clearly a political decision, though the department certainly agreed considerable advertising was needed. The department was satisfied that the content of the advertisements and related material was non-partisan and genuinely informative.

Our strategic plan usually highlighted communications as a 'key results area' for effective management of the department. We then had a complementary communications plan, which identified the broad policy approach and infrastructure we needed (for example, corporate image and badging, profile, web site role, ministerial correspondence arrangements, research, information, public relations skills) and the mandatory processes for specific communications strategies around, for example, any major government initiative.

During my time, the department did not conduct its own regular market research on public attitudes to its programs or administration. I can see a case for that for agencies in the business of directly delivering services, but am also mindful that it would be easy to cross the line in providing the governing party with privileged information that might be used for partisan purposes. We did, however, use market research extensively in most communications strategies for specific initiatives.

With the advent of the Internet, departmental web sites have become critical to the communications effort. Departments have learned that these sites require more effort than being a dump for their hardcopy publications and have invested in clever architecture and sometimes more active two-way communications through online, almost real-time exchanges, complementing ministerial and departmental correspondence. This has also led to the development of rules to separate departmental from ministerial sites, to preserve the political neutrality of departments and careful design to dampen expectations of unrealistic speed, accuracy and comprehensiveness of responses to individual queries.

Speeches and publications

I always took the view that one of the roles of a secretary was to make public speeches to explain the background to government policies and to promote informed discussion of the issues involved, without either directly promoting the government's policies or undermining them. I similarly favoured publications by the department disseminating facts about the programs, presenting departmental research and canvassing some of the more technical issues underpinning policies and programs. These served the department as well as external players and the public, by forcing a discipline on our analysis and opening our work up to external, expert examination.

Table 9.2 Health Occasional Papers

Between 1997 and 1999, the Health department issued five papers in its first series of Occasional Papers. These covered:

- national leadership through performance assessment
- family and community services: when is competition the answer
- a healthy start for zero to five year olds
- compression of morbidity workshop papers
- an overview of health status, health care and public health in Australia.

I was keen to promote more informed discussion of health financing issues generally and advised the minister on a number of occasions that some form of public inquiry or review would be helpful, perhaps by the Productivity Commission (notwithstanding my initial opposition to its 1996 inquiry into private health insurance). He took a more cautious

---

view, fearful that this could set hares running and reduce his capacity to manage the policy agenda. When he again rejected my proposal after the 1998 election, I decided the department might take some action to fill the gap, albeit without advocating any policy directions either generally or specifically.

It was a delicate matter, but it did lead to an excellent special series of Health Financing Occasional Papers, prepared under the leadership of one of the deputy secretaries, David Borthwick. The papers published between 1998 and 2000 included:

- Health financing in Australia: the objectives and players
- International approaches to funding health care
- Health expenditure: its management and sources
- Public and private: in partnership for Australia's health
- Technology, health and health care
- The quality of Australian health care: current issues and future directions
- *Health financing and population health.*

Another occasional paper on health financing, *Reforming the Australian health care system: the role of government*, was also issued in 1999, but was not formally part of this series.

The papers received many plaudits, including from Ross Gittins in the *Sydney Morning Herald*, and caused no political damage. Their existence, however, did require some resilience by me and the department in the face of some unease among the political staffers.

Freedom of information

The secretary may also become personally involved in managing FOI applications when they involve politically sensitive information. I delegated authority under the legislation, but was occasionally drawn in either by a delegate or (more often) by the minister or minister's office. I did not ever withdraw a delegation, but I might have sought clarification from the delegate of his or her assessment of the case for or against release.

Ministers and their advisers are understandably concerned to minimise political damage and do not always appreciate public service advice on the requirements of the legislation or common law understandings of the public interest where that is a factor (for example, internal working documents may not be released only if it is not in the public interest not to do so). Sometimes, however, they do understand that delaying the inevitable often exacerbates the problem.

Table 9.3 FOI can become very personal

I was accompanying Michael Wooldridge on a visit to the United States when, on the way to an important meeting one morning, he turned to me in the car blasting me about the department betraying him and lying to his office. I had no idea what he was on about until the adviser explained that it concerned an FOI request. The department overnight had released information requested about the minister's personal expenses in the form of all the various receipts for expenditure. The media back home was having a field day about such things as champagne with the AMA president after settling some negotiated agreement.

I contacted my office and sought the background. The minister remained furious all day, convinced of the department's disloyalty and unilateral action. Having finally obtained the full story, I went to the minister's hotel room late in the evening, a bottle of red wine (bought with my own money) under my arm. The staffer was with him.

I accepted responsibility for the department not forewarning the minister or his office of the precise time the information would be released, but advised that his office was aware of the request and the information to be released. I also noted that the FOI request followed the minister's continued refusal to answer a related Question on Notice, a reply to which we had drafted on several occasions.

The minister was not much mollified (given the continuing media fun and games), but said he appreciated my gesture and accepted it was my role to defend the department. I bit my tongue, waiting until the staffer and I had left his room to hand the adviser copies of all the emails I had. These detailed the extent of communication between the department and the office over several weeks, including the collation and verification of documents by the office, consideration of what had to be released under the law and the deadlines under the law for release. I told the staffer: 'You now know what I did not tell the minister: I could have nailed you and the office on this. There was no lying by the department or any disloyalty to the minister. You guys clearly did not keep the minister informed.'

Perhaps I should have been more forceful with the minister, but this way I won important credit with the office and greater cooperation from then on. I doubt the minister forgave us, however.

Direct contact with journalists

The department's standard rules were that contacts with the media would be referred to the public affairs area and/or the minister's office. By agreement with the office, some matters would be handled by the department, particularly if they were merely factual or related to a matter of administration or professional expertise where the general line to be used had been discussed with the office. For example, the Chief Medical Officer frequently commented publicly on public health and medical issues and the departmental delegate making a decision under a law might be the one to announce and explain the decision if there was media interest. Any policy matters or sensitive administrative matters would be handled by the minister's office.

Notwithstanding these rules, which I established in line with ministerial directions, I occasionally spoke directly to journalists without formal clearance. Generally, this was with journalists seeking background to current issues rather than information for an immediate news story. For example, I had conversations with Ross Gittins on the analysis behind the lifetime cover reform to private health insurance. Background conversations with journalists occurred up to once or twice a month, but mostly much less often. (I had many years earlier developed a good relationship with Gittins, who was keen to understand the background to policy decisions on social welfare as well as economics; he never betrayed the trust between us.)

More problematic were the calls from reporters such as Michelle Grattan on a breaking, high-profile story. These I ducked as a rule, though on occasions, again, I provided some background, particularly for follow-up commentary columns. (Grattan also never betrayed my trust, but her focus on politics made any contacts more risky.)

Differences of approach

Health has a much larger load in dealing with the media than most portfolios. It receives more headlines that it must respond to, its programs affect every member of the public and it has responsibilities in health promotion. Other line agencies might have smaller workloads, but most are involved in each of the elements I have described. Agencies directly delivering services are these days very extensively involved in sophisticated communications management, including through the use of the latest technology.

The central agencies' role varies. The Department of PM&C has the job of monitoring the media across all government activities and providing the Prime Minister with briefings on any of them. They, however, have limited involvement in broader communications management. Treasury under the Howard Government was drawn into preparing more briefs for the Treasurer than in the past, but the load on the Finance department seemed still to be relatively light.

Some departments are expected to deal directly with the media more often than others, perhaps related to the operational nature of the work (for example, the departments of Defence, Foreign Affairs) or to their expert roles, which are almost statutorily independent (for example, the Treasury Secretary).

More important, however, are the attitude of the minister and the personal style of the secretary. Ken Henry (Treasury Secretary) evidently has more licence from his minister under the Rudd Government and is a confident public speaker, but his public role is still a long way from John Stone's regular and frank briefing of the press in the 1970s and early 1980s. In my time, the secretaries who most often made public speeches were Allan Hawke (Defence), Peter Shergold and I.

Recent changes: the 24/7 news cycle

As mentioned, the power and reach of the media have increased dramatically during the past 40 years and, in response, the professionalism of the political process has grown, leading to greater control and increased sophistication of communications management. The relentless constancy of media attention—the 24/7 news cycle—now demands enormous resources and skills in government, which secretaries help to marshal and manage.

Technological developments in the communications field have also changed the way programs are managed.

Politics and the media have always been intertwined, with politicians sensitive about public servants' public statements and public servants usually favouring anonymity. Anonymity is harder to maintain nowadays, while the task of communications management is too great to be left entirely to the political arm of government.

Issues arising

The key issue is the respective role of the political and administrative arms. Ministers are concerned to maintain closer control and that control is increasingly centralised around the Prime Minister and his office. There is nonetheless a major role for the administrative arm as part of program management, as well as lending legitimate support to ministers.

Excessive political control can constrain the capacity of public servants to serve the public interest in making information available, publishing documents and giving speeches. The Public Service also needs to take care not to have its communications resources devoted to partisan purposes. As mentioned, market research in particular can be used for partisan purposes and secretaries need to be confident that taxpayer funding for such research is justified and can be defended in Senate Estimates hearings.

A particular case in point concerns the sensitivities around senior public servants speaking directly to journalists: few do it nowadays and those who do, do so less frequently and less openly. Similarly, secretaries make fewer public speeches these days than in the past. I think this is unfortunate, while agreeing firmly that care is needed not to betray the minister's trust and accepting there is a risk of misrepresentation by the media in order to create controversy. (I also believe it is wise for secretaries to try to avoid a high media profile, so that I do not favour them appearing before the National Press Club.) Seeking permission every time is also not really sensible: it can lead to unnecessarily cautious responses. While I have been pretty cautious, I believe secretaries should draw on their experience and judgment, recognising there is public interest in helping to explain government policies and to provide impartially some of the underlying analysis and research. Ministers should also recognise the professional standing and experience of their departmental secretaries and allow them some latitude on the understanding there will be discussion between them on handling politically sensitive matters.

Nonetheless, there is no easy answer here and sometimes even the most carefully considered comments to the media can blow up into political embarrassments. That is why some secretaries are just not willing to take any risk. My preferred approach, which occasionally got me into trouble when the media misused or exploited my comments or speeches, was just to wear it and move on, learning from the experience about who to trust and when and how to speak. I suspect most ministers and their staffers, however, would prefer a more cautious approach.

Table 9.4 Caught between a rock and a hard place

I accept I made an error of judgment at a late stage of the MRI scandal and yet I am still unwilling to shoulder all the blame.

Minister Wooldridge had tabled a statutory declaration by a departmental officer to support his statements that he had not divulged unauthorised information at a meeting with radiologists shortly before the 1998 budget. A radiologist subsequently wrote to the officer noting an omission in the declaration about his own presence at the meeting. I informed the minister.

Sometime later, a journalist and photographer camped outside my officer's home, evidently aware of the problem with the statutory declaration. I rang the journalist to ask him to back off, that it was unfair to put a public servant under such media pressure. He agreed to do so if I would answer his questions: was I aware of the error in the statutory declaration and had I informed the minister.

I said yes to both questions and then immediately rang the minister's office. The front-page story the next day reported my answers and the minister's failure at that point to correct the parliamentary record. The minister and his office felt I had been more keen to protect my staff than to support the minister. I can see their point and agree I should have rung them first, but had I done so the story would have been essentially the same, and appeared the same day, and with no less prominence, and the officer would have been under unfair public exposure and criticism as well.

Table 9.5 Slaps on the wrist

After the government introduced the 30 per cent rebate on private health insurance premiums, I was invited to speak at a public conference of private health insurance and private hospital executives in Canberra. I gave the conference participants some background to the government's policies on private health and Medicare, noting how important it was that the industry also took action to ensure its members got value for money and used competition among hospitals to do so. If they did not, and premiums again began to increase, the benefits from the new rebate would be put at risk.

The speech seemed to be well received and follow-up questions were sensible. There were no press stories for about a week. *The Australian* then decided to give it a beat-up with a headline that I was questioning the merits of the rebate.

The Prime Minister's Office called me directly to ask whether the speech had been cleared by the minister and accusing me of improperly speaking on behalf of the government. I had not formally cleared the speech, but had sent a copy to the minister before it was delivered. The minister later told me it was a good speech, as it was important to put some responsibility back on the industry. The journalist rang to apologise for the headline on the story, but I was under no illusion: the view of the Prime Minister's Office was that secretaries should not give public speeches unless formally cleared by ministers beforehand, and even then they were frowned on.

A related issue concerns how proactive media management should be. I recall a presentation at one portfolio secretaries' retreat by a former Fairfax executive, which included the advice that governments (and departments) should supply positive news stories to crowd out negative stories. Health was cited as an example, where the public interest in health led to the allocation of considerable space and time by media outlets to stories of interest, which, if not filled with interesting material on medical breakthroughs or heart-warming stories of selflessness or courage or success through adversity, would be filled with stories of crises and hospital errors and so on. Some politicians and their media advisers might play that sort of game, but most of us were not persuaded that this would be consistent with the values of the Public Service.

The popular image already is that communications management is more often about spin than substance. The image might be a caricature, but nonetheless represents a real issue. Apart from the need for communications management not to be partisan (for example, through the level or nature of taxpayer-funded advertising and research), it is important not to allow media management to lead to excessive focus on short-term populist measures and insufficient consideration of the longer-term public interest and options that might serve that interest.

It is here that the media can be simplistic and self-interested. There is public interest in some limits to access to information. Politicians might try to press this too far, but equally the media often does not acknowledge the public interest in government having reasonable time and space, without the public constantly looking over its shoulder, to consider complex issues, canvass options widely, have frank discussion within the bounds of collective responsibility and receive frank and fearless advice from officials and political advisers. The press rarely if ever condemns someone who leaks confidential information, notwithstanding the breach of trust involved, and seems unable to recognise the irony of its own insistence on preserving the anonymity of its sources of information.

Secretaries, however, need to be careful to ensure decisions on access to information are made according to the law. If they or their officers hold the delegation, they must make their own judgments as delegates weighing up the public interest where appropriate without direction from ministers. In my time, I saw too many secretaries spend too much time trying to please their ministers by exploiting exemptions under the *FOI Act* or not keeping records, rather than acting with genuine impartiality and in the public interest.

Ministers are understandably uncomfortable about revelations, through FOI requests or other processes, of advice they have not accepted, which proves to have been sound or of events or reports that are embarrassing and hard to explain. Several warned me on occasions that public access to departmental advice would lead them to insisting on advice being oral only with no records that could be subject to FOI requests. I never took this too seriously, though no doubt I did dampen the forcefulness of some of my written advice and the tenor of records of some discussions in more recent years. I do not believe the courts systematically undervalue the public interest in keeping certain deliberations confidential; more likely is that ministers, and their public service advisers, undervalue the public interest in openness.

Table 9.6 Legal options to limit FOI versus legal obligations to create and maintain records

A meeting of all departmental secretaries in 2004 discussed concerns about the media campaign, led by *The Australian* newspaper, to challenge decisions (including the issuing of 'final certificates') to exempt documents from FOI. Discussion focused first on the definition of 'documents' and then, when the meeting was advised by Rob Cornall (Secretary of the Attorney-General's department) that the legislation implied a wide definition, discussion turned to ways of limiting the number of documents held that were not unequivocally exempt from public release. Keeping diaries was firmly discouraged, those with 'day books' or similar were advised to destroy them at the end of each week or fortnight and it was suggested that good practice was to systematically review document holdings to destroy draft papers that were no longer essential for future work. Where possible, policy documents were to be managed as cabinet papers, which were exempt.

One secretary went so far as to boast that he never kept written records of conversations with the minister, but reported back to his departmental officers orally on decisions made and action to be taken.

Cornall was asked to provide further legal advice on how to gain exemptions from FOI coverage.

I expressed concern that the conversation was so one-sided. I noted the Auditor-General had frequently criticised the lack of adequate record keeping and asked Cornall to give us legal advice also on the obligations of public servants to make and to keep records. Cornall agreed that this was a sensible request. (As I recall, the subsequent advice provided was that there was no explicit obligation to create records, though the *Public Service Act* and the *Financial Management and Accountability Act* arguably implied some such obligation—for example, through the value of 'open accountability'; the *Archives Act* certainly constrained the destruction of records once created.)

I also asked the secretary who claimed he did not keep records how he expected his staff to carry out the minister's decisions, which he had relayed orally. Surely effective management, let alone the obligation of accountability, meant someone would make a record of the decisions.

A year later, when I was working in the Department of PM&C, I was intrigued by the systematic trawling of files, official and unofficial, to destroy 'surplus' copies of draft papers and other papers not essential for recording the decision-making process. There were also systematic

> arrangements to tie as much policy advice to cabinet papers as possible. The processes did not involve the destruction of any key documents, but were clearly aimed at limiting the risk of FOI (or parliamentary) requests for working papers being upheld.

A less significant but fascinating management issue in communications and media relations is handling the culture of good public affairs staff. The fact is, the best such staff are not like traditional public servants. They are often extroverts, do not like rules and processes, abhor authority, cut corners and speak out of turn. Any attempt to corral them, however, let alone replace them with classical bureaucrats, runs the risk of losing their creativity and effectiveness in their jobs. I tried, not always successfully, to give the public affairs unit some licence under the leadership of an older, more experienced person with media nous. On a couple of occasions, things went badly and I had to pursue disciplinary action against individuals who misused resources, but on the one occasion (in the Housing department) when I intervened more forcefully to impose much firmer controls, the downside was far worse, with the loss of several of my most talented and creative people.

Lessons learned

It is important to gain the minister's confidence in the department's handling of communications and this requires having a capable unit in the department that works closely with the minister's office. Having rules requiring everything to be cleared through the minister's office is not good practice in my view, and is certainly not a sign of confidence in the department.

Secretaries need a thick skin, particularly in departments such as Health, where stories of scandals and crises happen every day. They also need, however, political antennae to judge the stories that are likely to 'run' and require high-level, careful responses and management.

Secretaries also need access to expertise within and outside the department in communications management, including in the best use of new technology. A big part of the secretary's role is to clarify the integrity standards involved, particularly regarding political neutrality and value for money.

It is important for secretaries to give public speeches from time to time, particularly in large and complex portfolios where policies and programs need more public explanation than can ever be delivered by ministers. It is also important to maintain publications of research and statistics and background policy analysis. If the minister is not comfortable with this, alternatives need to be found, such as contracted research (with some independent capacity to publish) or the use of a statutory honest broker (such as the AIHW). Confidential discussions with external experts and stakeholders are useful but not sufficient, in my view, either to ensure departmental advice is well informed or to ensure public understanding of the issues.

Secretaries also have a role to play at times in speaking directly to journalists. I am not sure it is wise to seek permission formally to do so as the official answer is likely to be unnecessarily restrictive. There is, however, a risk of such discussions going wrong and hence of undermining the confidence of the minister.

Looking forward, I suspect this is an area for more careful review and guidance. The Public Service Commissioner has issued more and very useful guidance in the area since I left the service, but I am not sure it recognises sufficiently the public interest in public access to the expertise and experience of public servants whether through departmental publications or through occasional background briefing, not managed directly by ministers. Public interest would not be served if this access led to loss of confidence of ministers in their departments.

10. Dead poet society duties: promoting APS values and contributing to APS capability

Elements of this role

Agency heads have a statutory obligation to promote as well as uphold the APS Values, many of which can be traced back to the Northcote Trevelyan Report of 1854, which established the Westminster tradition of a professional, non-partisan career public service. All portfolio secretaries and heads of some other large agencies are also members of the Management Advisory Committee, which is a statutory body under the *Public Service Act*. This reflects an obligation on secretaries that goes beyond their management of departments to contribute to improved management practices throughout the APS and to strengthening APS capability.

Secretaries meet this obligation in a number of ways:

- by ensuring their own staff are imbued with the APS Values and identify themselves with a cohesive, highly professional APS
- by participating actively in cross-APS activities such as the MAC and APS Commission forums
- by supporting APS-wide career management and succession management for senior public servants
- by participating in external forums such as the Australia New Zealand School of Government (ANZSOG) and the Institute of Public Administration Australia (IPAA), which foster public service professionalism.

Promoting the APS Values

I invested quite heavily in a values-based approach to building cohesion in each of the departments I led, strengthening relationships within and beyond the organisation and promoting ethical behaviour. It was not until I became Public Service Commissioner, however, that I fully appreciated the connection between the values I had been espousing and the APS Values that I had been required by statute to promote. The connection had always been there: indeed, in health, we explicitly referred to the APS Values in our strategic plan as well as the values we were giving particular priority to in pursuing our business objectives, and I do not doubt that staff understood the priority I personally gave to public service professionalism.

Perhaps the most successful initiative was the 'Fork in the Road Café' ethics awareness campaign we ran in the Department of Health. It was developed by some very innovative staff, including Andrew Wood and Michelle Kinnane (Table 10.1).

Fork-in-the-Road Cafe hypothetical: Geoffrey Robertson with (visible) Senator Grant Tambling, Professor Don Chalmers, Louise Dodson, David Graham, Peter Sekuless, Dr Barry Catchlove and Andrew Podger (photo by kind permission of the Department of Health and Ageing)

Table 10.1 'Fork in the Road Café'

This was the title of the ethics awareness campaign we ran in the Department of Health from 2000. The title reflected the basic lesson: when facing a dilemma, stop (in the café) and reflect, discussing it with respected colleagues and checking guidelines and precedents, before making a decision. All staff attended half-day workshops over about 12 months; subsequently, the program was a compulsory element of induction training for all new staff.

The purpose was to promote the values of public service professionalism in the environment of greater devolution and fewer specific rules. The campaign encouraged discussion of common workplace dilemmas, using a 'hypothetical' video commissioned from Geoffrey Robertson (and starring Senator Tambling, various departmental officers, a top journalist and a newspaper editor, an industry lobbyist and a CEO of a private sector chain of health services).

Issues canvassed included conflict of interest, ethical research, working with industry, whistleblowing, post-separation employment, leaking, gifts and entertainment, and non-partisanship.

The campaign later influenced APS Commission programs promoting values and ethics awareness.

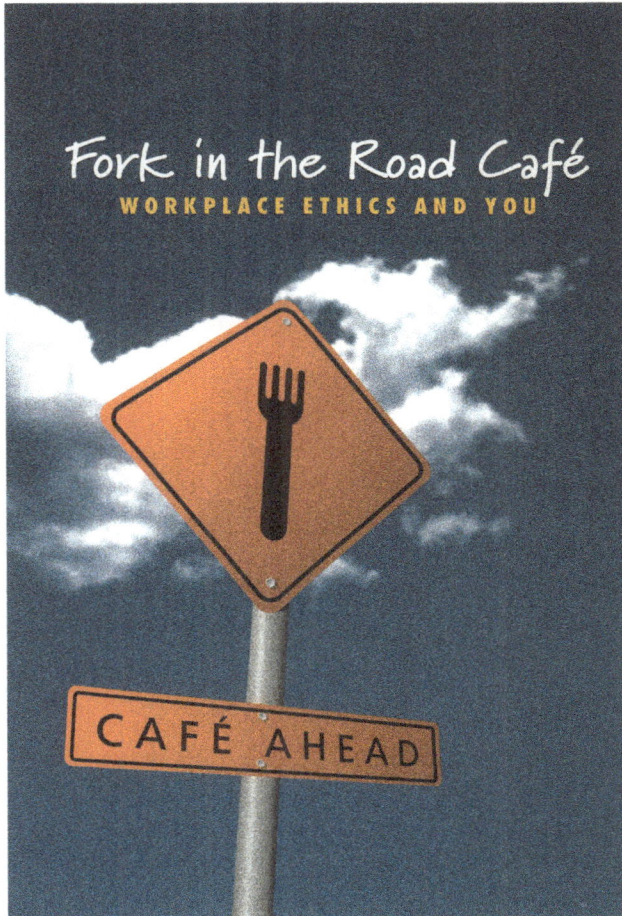

Participating in cross-APS activities

The Secretary of the Department of PM&C chaired a monthly portfolio secretaries' meeting and MAC meetings three or four times a year. He also hosted a two-day retreat each year, held in Sydney since about 1997, at the Reserve Bank facility opposite the Prime Minister's residence in Kirribilli. The Secretary of the Department of Employment and Workplace Relations also chaired a monthly meeting of agency heads to discuss industrial relations issues. The portfolio secretaries' meetings focused mainly on immediate operational issues requiring coordination throughout the government, often emanating directly from the Prime Minister or cabinet. The retreat focused mainly on some major medium-term policy challenges affecting most portfolios, though the former occasionally addressed some urgent or sensitive management issues (such as running costs and secretaries' pay and conditions) and the latter also always had one session devoted to management issues (including, in most years, some discussion of SES career management).

The main formal forums for discussing APS-wide management and capability issues are the MAC and the Employment Secretary's meetings of agency heads (effectively, a workplace relations committee). The MAC projects always progressed under a reference group of interested secretaries, with a project team of deputies. The secretaries' contribution was sometimes quite substantial in time and intellectual content. The APS Commission also pursues many of its responsibilities for promoting leadership and improved management through informal forums of secretaries, and secretaries also frequently make presentations at APS Commission leadership development programs, particularly those aimed at new SES officers. The APS Commission's activities, including through the MAC, are described in more detail in Chapter 12.

The Employment Secretary's workplace relations committee meetings provided an important forum for considering industrial relations issues and also aspects of capability, including attraction and retention of skilled staff and ideas for productivity enhancement. They were not always successful. Under the Howard Government's industrial relations policies, agency heads ostensibly had far greater flexibility in managing pay and conditions, but the Employment department retained authority to approve enterprise bargaining agreements and also enthusiastically pursued its interpretation of government policy on individual employment contracts (AWAs). The real risk of devolution pushing up wages as agencies competed with each other required not only the discipline of budget constraints but having agency heads exchange information on their proposed enterprise agreements, including productivity offsets. These meetings helped to ensure such information exchange but the ideological direction might have been avoided had the commissioner, or even the Secretary of the Department of PM&C, chaired the meetings (my view remains that the commission should have responsibility for overall guidance on public service pay and conditions).

I was an active participant in all these forums whatever my agency head role. I made a substantial submission to Ron McLeod's review of the *Public Service Act* in 1995 when in the Housing department, participated in several of Helen Williams' reference groups when in the Health department, led or contributed substantially to MAC reviews and APS Commission studies in my role as commissioner (see Chapter 12) and participated actively in the workplace relations committee throughout the Howard Government years.

APS-wide career management

Tony Ayers promoted the view that in every large department at least one of the deputies should be clearly destined to be a secretary in the future. I accepted this view and always endeavoured to have in at least one of my deputies someone who would gain from the experience in order to help them as a future secretary. They must have won the deputy position on merit, but whenever I had a vacancy I would canvass with the Public Service Commissioner and some fellow secretaries possible candidates for transfer as well as promotion who were serious options as future secretaries and would benefit from experience in my department.

Table 10.2 Grooming secretaries

While some critics have claimed that the frequency of secretary appointments among those with executive experience in the departments of PM&C or Finance reflects power battles in the service, or policy capture by neo-liberals, the truth is that it reflects conscious career planning by individuals and succession management by senior secretaries.

I had the privilege of working in the departments of PM&C and Finance, as well as many other agencies, particularly in the social policy field. Among those I worked with in PM&C in the late 1970s were Ian Castles, David Charles, Michael Codd, John Enfield, Neville Stephens and Ed Visbord. Among those I worked with in finance in the 1980s were Pat Barrett, Tony Blunn, Neil Johnston, Michael Keating, David Rosalky, Steve Sedgwick and Helen Williams.

Following Tony Ayers' views on the responsibilities of all secretaries to help in the development of future secretaries, I negotiated the transfer of David Borthwick from Treasury to health as one of my deputies with Ted Evans, ensuring he gained experience in an operational agency (and I gained his considerable economic expertise). I had previously promoted Jeff Harmer to join me as a deputy in housing, and later was pleased when Lynelle Briggs joined me in health as a division head on transfer from social security: both were regarded by me as potential future secretaries. (Future secretaries and agency heads Jane Halton and Lisa Paul also worked with me in health and Jeff Whalan in housing, but, while I hope I contributed to their development, they were in those departments when I arrived).

Tony Ayers was also mentor to an extraordinarily wide range of public servants across the whole service. I never matched his achievements in this respect, but I did accept responsibility before and after appointment as a secretary to maintain contact with officers who had worked with me in different agencies. I followed their careers with interest and provided advice if asked on their options for future development and work. These networks also helped me from time to time to understand broader policy debates and service-wide management issues.

External professional development

Most secretaries also encouraged involvement by their staff in external professional development that reinforced their broader APS role and contribution. As a rule, the President of the ACT Division of the Institute of Public Administration Australia (IPAA) is a current departmental secretary or agency head. I was president for two years when in the Health department. Secretaries often speak at IPAA forums such as the national conference and noteworthy speeches at these or other forums are regularly published in the IPAA's journals. In whichever agency I managed, I was a more frequent speaker and author than most.

Michael Wooldridge presenting Andrew Podger (Health Secretary and IPAA ACT President) with the Annual Reports Award for 1997 (photo by kind permission of the Department of Health and Ageing)

Other professional associations that I saw contribute substantially to the broad development of public servants in different agencies included the Economics Society, the Australian Institute of Management, the Australian Human Resources Institute, the Australian Project Management Association and the Australian College of Health Service Executives.

The establishment of the Australia New Zealand School of Government (ANZSOG) in 2004 has provided a stronger base for developing leaders in Australasian jurisdictions. I was a member of the inaugural board, but many other secretaries contributed to the creation of ANZSOG and then to its programs by making regular appearances.

Differences in approach

Obviously, the Public Service Commissioner and the Secretary of the Department of PM&C have more direct responsibilities for building the capability of the APS as a whole than other agency heads, but even their contribution varies with the personalities of the individuals involved. Max Moore-Wilton was less active, for example, than Michael Keating as chair of the MAC (or its predecessor, the Management Advisory Board); Peter Shergold's appointment led to some reinvigoration of the MAC.

The contribution of other secretaries and agency heads varies considerably according to personal interests and styles. The majority in my time were genuinely interested and committed, but the time they could devote to MAC or APS Commission activities was often limited. Some invested a great deal of time and energy. A few were less interested, viewing the commission and even the MAC as costly overheads that did not add much value to their particular businesses. The Department of Foreign Affairs and Trade (DFAT) at times seemed to see themselves as an elite, even a separate foreign service (reflecting a long history), demonstrated by the explicit view of the then secretary Ashton Calvert that, while they had many top candidates for departmental secretary jobs in the APS, no non-DFAT person could ever be a candidate for head of DFAT (or even a senior diplomatic post) unless forced on them via 'political' appointments (even Allan Hawke's appointment as High Commissioner to New Zealand was described by Calvert as 'political' and his capabilities were undervalued). One or two others simply did not value the institution of the Public Service sufficiently to invest time or effort in cross-service activities (other than policy work that enhanced their exposure to ministers and the Prime Minister).

Interestingly, some agency heads outside *Public Service Act* coverage were important contributors and allies. These included, for example, Mick Keelty from the Australian Federal Police and Dennis Richardson from the Australian Security Intelligence Organisation (ASIO).

Changes over time

Under new public management in the 1980s and 1990s, devolution was accompanied by substantial networking, through the Management Advisory Board and its Management Improvement Advisory Committee and other informal groups, to promote improved financial management and, subsequently, broader management. Financial management capability within and across agencies improved significantly, even if people-management improvements lagged somewhat. Enthusiasm for this concerted APS-wide learning waned in the late 1990s as devolution was pressed further and the Secretary of the Department of PM&C showed less interest in the subject. The Finance department, too, withdrew from its former leadership position and the APS Commission struggled a little to gain support in the absence of other central agency leadership.

Nonetheless, my strong impression is that, despite some ups and downs, agencies' investment in training their own staff increased substantially during the 1990s.

More recently, the issue of public service capability has been reinvigorated not only in the APS but in other Australasian jurisdictions, most obviously through the establishment of ANZSOG. This began in the Howard Government years, with Moore-Wilton lending his support to Victoria's suggestion to establish ANZSOG and with Shergold and Ian Watt pressing the capability agenda further as they took up their roles as head of the departments of PM&C and Finance respectively, supporting the Public Service Commissioner's advocacy.

This renewed interest was the result not only of recognition that the previous focus on individual agencies alone was sometimes counterproductive as agencies competed with each other in a tightening labour market and was also constraining capacity to deliver whole-of-government initiatives. It also reflected a growing realisation that greater workforce mobility, an ageing workforce and increasingly complex demands on managers required a different approach to capability building than the traditional 'apprenticeship'-type model in which public servants learned through osmosis on the job at the feet of their elders. Instead, public services need to invest more in continuing formal learning covering technical, management and leadership skills, and cross-agency and cross-jurisdiction learning and networking are essential.

This new emphasis is not replacing the investment by each agency in its own capability building; it is complementing and reinforcing that investment. Across public services, I am sure investment in capability building is now substantially higher than in the 1980s and early 1990s, within agencies and service-wide.

Values and capability issues

The APS Values are open to interpretation. I am somewhat of a traditionalist, wedded to Westminster principles of a professional service serving the elected government loyally but with a measure of independence through obligations to be apolitical and impartial. As in the film of that name, this enthusiasm for a 'dead poets' society' was not just nostalgia for an arcane past, but a living philosophy of 'seizing the day' to serve the public. This view emphasises the shared culture and common role of the Public Service as a whole and the importance of nurturing the service and continually building and diversifying its overall capability.

Others have somewhat different views. Some give more weight to the different businesses of different agencies, focusing their attention more exclusively on their own agencies and complaining about central agency requirements. Some see closer similarities with the private sector, where investment in capability must deliver adequate rates of return, preferably in quantifiable terms such as the amount or price of agency outputs. Some give more weight to being responsive to the immediate demands of the government of the day and less to the requirement for a degree of professional independence or to the capability of the service as a whole to support future governments.

Perhaps the key shift in the values and culture of the Public Service in the past 30 years is the greater emphasis on performance—in delivering services ('management for results') and in serving the government ('responsiveness'). For some secretaries, at least for a while, this reduced the importance of service-wide approaches to capability building and narrowed their interpretation of their obligation to promote the APS Values.

The renewed interest in service-wide approaches has also been associated with a shift towards greater engagement with external groups and organisations and the importance of enhancing capability to respond to and manage change and uncertainty.

The main practical issue for secretaries has been in balancing their efforts to enhance their organisations' capabilities to meet their business requirements now and into the future and their contribution to broader APS and public sector capability. This is not a simple either/or issue, but a question of supporting both to the extent time and money are available.

My own view is that it should be mandatory for the SES, as the leadership cadre of the APS, to undertake key APS Commission programs of leadership development and management improvement. The quid pro quo, however, is close involvement of agency heads in the design and performance feedback of the programs.

A related issue is the power or influence of the APS Commission and Department of PM&C Secretary in SES succession management, including movement of deputy secretaries to enhance the readiness of people for future agency head positions. I am inclined to the view that our approach is a little too laissez faire.

Another related issue concerns the extent of joint actions in areas such as recruitment and induction training. My inclination is for agency heads to continue to have the freedom to work independently or collaboratively, but for the APS Commission to facilitate collaboration for those who favour that. I found in the Health department that there was benefit in a recruitment strategy that combined targeting those interested specifically in health careers with working also to gain our fair share of those looking more generally to public service employment through the broad, collaborative recruitment process coordinated by the APS Commission. Health tended not to attract the very best among the latter when candidates nominated their preferred agency, but the field of those specifically interested in health omitted many capable generalists with considerable potential to contribute to the Department of Health and the broader Public Service.

The IPAA plays an important role as a professional association. It has a degree of independence in its support of professionalism among those involved in public administration whatever their level or role, but it also serves jurisdictions and their public service leadership as a forum for informed debate and study of current issues, drawing together practitioners and academics. Several IPAA divisions also provide extensive training opportunities to middle managers in particular. The support of the IPAA by departmental secretaries is essential, as is their willingness to tolerate if not encourage open debate and fearless evaluation of public administration policies and practices. Other associations also provide valuable professional development services and opportunities and rely on the support of secretaries and other senior managers.

Lessons learned

Contributing to APS-wide capability, and broader public sector capability, is a core responsibility of all secretaries. It might not be an explicit responsibility, but it is implicit through membership of the MAC and through the obligation to promote as well as uphold the APS Values. A few lost sight of this periodically.

Secretaries contribute in part, simply by the example of their own behaviour, demonstrating their support of cross-agency cooperation and collaboration.

They can also contribute directly by personal contributions to such capability-enhancing activities as MAC projects, helping to develop processes or practices or to promote investments and structures that will improve the future performance of the service. Cooperating on recruitment and staff development, and promoting and participating in SES leadership programs and mentoring staff beyond the secretary's own department, can make a major impact on overall capacity and the cohesion of the service.

Each secretary accepting this responsibility is not, however, sufficient. Central agency heads, particularly the secretaries of the departments of PM&C and Finance, need to take a leadership role along with the APS Commission in sponsoring and promoting networks that encourage improvements in leadership capabilities and management skills, and in capacity in policy analysis and advice. They are also in key positions to ensure adequate investment in cross-service processes and systems including interoperable databases, shared recruitment and development and linked reporting systems.

Informal approaches to enhancing capability also increasingly need to be complemented by formal training and development given trends in labour market supply and complexity of work requirements. Much of this also requires shared investment—ANZSOG being a model that might be extended into particular fields such as health, education and industry regulation.

11. Secretaries' personal development, support and performance assessment

Elements

Secretaries and other agency heads are all individuals with their own personal histories and personal styles and habits. Nonetheless, there are common skills and capabilities required for these jobs that need to be developed and nurtured, and their application supported and assessed. This chapter is a little more personal than the others, reflecting my own background and style, while also attempting to draw out issues and lessons. It canvasses:

- career planning and development
- continuing professional development
- personal support
- performance assessment.

Career planning and development

Australia does not have a formal, structured approach to grooming people for top public service positions, unlike practice in some other countries such as the United Kingdom and Singapore. Our approach is more laissez faire, relying almost entirely on personal career decisions and merit processes for selection to each and every position, at least up to the higher bands of the SES. This approach has been reinforced in recent times in response to increased mobility and increased lateral recruitment into the APS, including at SES and agency head levels.

There have, however, been influential schemes, particularly for young graduate recruits, whose impact on the senior echelons of the APS continues to the present. When I was a secretary, I was one of several former Australian Bureau of Statistics (ABS) cadets who were agency heads. Others included Michael Keating and Neil Johnston. There were many more in the 1980s (for example, Vince FitzGerald, Chris Higgins and Michael Codd). There are still at least three former administrative trainees among the current group of secretaries (Helen Williams, Andrew Metcalfe and Terry Moran); Allan Hawke and Roger Beale were others in my time. Ian Watt was a Treasury cadet.

These schemes did not so much groom people for future senior roles (though they did provide participants with excellent training), as recruit some of the best and brightest, encourage them to commit to a career in the APS and promote their ambitions for higher achievement. After a year or two of special treatment, the participants were left to their own devices to pursue their preferred career paths, and a remarkable number proved successful.

Most of my cohort of ABS cadets chose to leave the bureau a few years after coming to Canberra, having gained an interest in some area of policy with which they had become familiar through ABS statistical work; a few left the Public Service. In my case, I developed an interest in social policy and alleviation of poverty, having worked on the Henderson Poverty Inquiry surveys. The ABS cadetship certainly succeeded in convincing me to commit to an APS career, even though the bureau had my services for only about four years after my graduation. Some stayed in the bureau. One, Dennis Trewin, later became the Statistician, succeeding another former cadet, Bill McLennan.

My commitment to the Public Service strengthened during and directly after the Whitlam Government, as I studied public administration part-time at The Australian National University and as I was given remarkable opportunities for someone my age to advise on income security and welfare matters. I also matured greatly in my understanding of public service professionalism during this time. When I joined the Social Welfare Commission in 1974, I accepted the widely held view in the Whitlam Government of an antagonistic public service, but this was replaced during 1975 by a growing respect for the quality of the advice I saw emanating from the more traditional departments, Treasury, Social Security and the Prime Minister and Cabinet. Individuals such as Colin McAlister (Social Security), Sir William (then Bill) Cole (Treasury) and Ian Castles (PM&C), revealed to me a professionalism that served the government and involved rigorous analysis with frank and open debate among individual public servants and agencies. The revelation of the 'Loans affair' and the courageous advice from Sir Frederick Wheeler to Prime Minister Whitlam added to my appreciation of the value of a somewhat independent, professional public service. I was still keen to see reforms to the Public Service such as through greater public engagement and more understanding of disadvantaged Australians, and looked positively towards the report of the Coombs Royal Commission (the Royal Commission into Australian Government Administration), which reported in 1976.

Working in the Department of Social Security in the late 1970s, when Senator Margaret Guilfoyle was the minister, capped this stage of my development as her relationship with the department, and in particular with the Development Division where I worked, proved to be the most constructive and professional one that I experienced in my whole career.

My development was therefore primarily experiential, rather than based on formal training, though my studies at The Australian National University and reading of the Coombs Commission reports and papers gave me some good grounding in public administration history.

From time to time, there have been programs for the feeder group into the SES to help those with potential to build up their capacity through training and/or work experience. These schemes, such as the Executive Development Scheme (EDS), were effective for a while in identifying potential leaders and giving them broader experience, but they were never really focused on those expected to go to the top. They were more successful in helping those trapped in the system to find better career paths and maximise their potential. The Senior Women in Management (SWIM) scheme was particularly effective in this regard.

For the most part, serious consideration of people for top positions begins only when they are well entrenched in the SES with a proven record at that level. As I have described elsewhere, this is still managed in a light-touch way, with agency heads encouraged to consider succession management, and appropriate development of those with potential.

I was promoted early to the SES, in 1978, while only twenty-nine years old. This was not entirely unusual at that time given the then age structure of the service, with many post-World War II recruits nearing retirement, an explosion of recruitment in the late 1960s and early 1970s and enormous growth in Commonwealth programs and employment in the Whitlam era. Nonetheless, I had virtually no management experience and no management training, though I had established a reputation for policy analysis in income security in particular. Moreover, I was extremely sceptical of the advantages of management training of any sort and derided colleagues who employed such nerdy techniques as diaries; I believed I could manage anything on my ear.

I was terribly wrong, though I avoided being found out through any major disaster, partly because I had the continued good fortune of being among teams of very able individuals who did not need much managing, and who taught me subtly some basics such as supervision, research management and budget cycle planning, as well as applied policy skills such as drafting cabinet submissions and briefings (McAlister, my division head in the Department of Social Security, was particularly helpful as a coach). I also found I could draw on my policy skills not only to analyse issues but to reshape small teams to address what I saw as emerging priorities. In the Social Security department in the late 1970s, these included a stronger focus on tax and social security linkages and occupational superannuation, and moving away from the previous Whitlam Government's focus on national compensation and national superannuation.

When I moved to the Finance department in 1982, I was still cynical about management training, but began to learn much more on the job about financial management and managing a branch. On promotion to division head in the Finance department in 1986, I first started consciously to think about my management responsibilities. I had about 70 staff and responsibility for financial oversight of about six portfolios as well as public sector employment matters (for the Defence Force and the Public Service). I even engaged a consultant, Bill Godfrey, to help with some strategic planning for the division, which led us to focus on being in essence a consultancy business, with the capacity and flexibility to provide high-quality advice and scrutiny, responding quickly to emerging government priorities. We focused on such issues as our structure, our skills requirements and our relationships with agencies in our patch, as well as our budget and staff resources, which had been the main focus of earlier business planning. I suspect this was a first within the Finance department, although by then Finance was promoting financial management improvement throughout the APS.

Shortly afterwards, I attended my first ever management training. It changed my attitude to training completely.

Table 11.1 'Top management' training

The 1989 'Top Management' course was sponsored by the Public Service Commission and attended by Band 2 and 3 officers considered by their agency heads to have potential for top positions. It was my first ever management training course. The selection of participants was not bad, as it included half a dozen future secretaries (including Steve Sedgwick, Allan Hawke and Jo Hewitt) and a future Chief of the Navy (Rear Admiral Ian McDougall). The course included substantial material on strategic planning, with a case study by groups of participants on the future of Australian construction services and training in communications and media.

I kept the course material and my notes for the rest of my career, drawing on them in each new agency I joined. I finally understood that management skills could be learned through formal training and on-the-job experience and was not just something you developed with intelligence and the right personality.

With hindsight, I can now see the hidden guidance and career planning that was being orchestrated by some APS leaders, particularly the commission and the head of the Department of PM&C, but also by Tony Ayers and Michael Keating (then in the Finance department).

I first became very aware of this when I was approached by Ayers to apply to be a deputy secretary in the Defence department. There was no doubt his approach came after discussions with Keating and others, and reflected Ayers' interest in the Public Service as a whole, not just the Defence department.

Table 11.2 Informal career planning: lunch with Tony Ayers

In early 1990, Tony Ayers invited me to lunch to 'talk about my future'. I had worked with Ayers in Social Security, but we had separated somewhat unhappily in 1982 and had not had much interaction since. I was intrigued and agreed to meet him at his 'club', a Chinese restaurant in Yarralumla.

There he proposed that I apply for an impending deputy vacancy in the Department of Defence, in charge of capital procurement and logistics—perhaps the biggest management job for a deputy in the APS. I was stunned: I had limited management experience, limited understanding of defence and no technical expertise in engineering or project management.

Ayers felt that, with suitable support in the organisation, I could handle the job. He told me that Michael Keating considered I was the best manager in the Finance department and could draw on that in this much larger task. He was also looking for stronger financial discipline and probity in defence acquisitions.

Importantly, he spoke about my future career in the APS. He said I was likely to be approached to be a deputy in the Finance department in the next year or so, but accepting that would be a mistake. I already had nearly eight years in Finance and, if promoted again there, I might forever be perceived as a Finance person. His view was that I should be looking to move back into a line agency where I could make a greater contribution to public policy.

If I wanted to head a line department, however, I needed to learn a lot more about management. My management experience to date relied on knowing personally all my people and knowing personally the matters they were dealing with. I needed to learn how to manage when it was not physically possible to know everyone or to know all the subject matter. This required much greater skills in people management, in delegation of authority and in selective reporting and oversight.

So it was that later in 1990 I went to the Department of Defence and learned far more about management while (hopefully) contributing to defence capability not only during my four years in the department but for the next decade and more as projects such as over-the-horizon radar came into operation.

My first appointment as secretary was to the Department of Administrative Services and the Arts, where my main responsibilities were business and financial management. While excited by the challenges of the commercialisation agenda at the time and keen to see through the reforms, I was a little uneasy that I was destined now to be seen primarily as a manager, whereas I still desired to contribute to social policy. Such opportunities soon arose, perhaps a little too quickly (I was in this department for only four months before being moved to the Department of Housing and Regional Development).

Continuing professional development

Secretaries, like anyone else, need to maintain their professional capacity. I chose to remain actively involved in a number of professional associations, such as the IPAA, the Australian Institute of Management, the Economics Society and the Australian College of Health Service Executives. I participated regularly in seminars and conferences, as a speaker and, more importantly and more often, as a listener and learner.

On occasions, I arranged for the executive team to participate together in a management conference to consider possible new approaches and to strengthen our own ties.

I also had wonderful assistance from the agencies' librarians, particularly Titi Alexander, who moved to the Health department after the demise of the Department of Administrative Services, where we had first met. Alexander regularly checked with me my main interests and ensured I received relevant journal articles, book summaries and reviews, and so on, aware of my limited time to read much at length.

I never rose to the heights of Castles in keeping up with research in the professional fields I specialised in, but I still modelled my investment in continuing professional development on his approach and that of other secretaries I worked with who placed emphasis on keeping up with the research, such as Mike Keating, Neil Johnston, Ted Evans and Steve Sedgwick.

Personal support to the office of the secretary

Secretaries need considerable personal support to play their role effectively. This includes a personal secretary (or executive assistant). I was fortunate to have a series of quite excellent secretaries who were extraordinarily hardworking and dedicated and personally loyal. The role is complex and sensitive. There are the obvious duties of managing appointments, handling minor correspondence and preparing notes, managing papers and handling administration such as travel, all of which require particular competencies. Then there are the mostly unstated roles of:

- ensuring the secretary has quality time to think and read and write
- controlling access to the secretary without being seen to do so
- reflecting the style that the secretary wants presented to staff and clients.

Each of my secretaries had their own personalities, but all had a good sense of humour and the ability to present me and the office as open, with their role being to facilitate access, not limit it. They also knew it was important to convey a professional image to staff and to external stakeholders. They all served me well. My last secretary, Theresa Graham, worked with me in the Health department and the APS Commission, and subsequently in the Department of PM&C. Her style was understated, being approachable to all staff and never threatening, yet able quietly to help me discipline the allocation of my time. She is a treasure.

In large organisations, I found the need for a 'staff officer' or senior executive assistant, as well as a secretary. I learned this in the Defence department, where two and three-star officers in particular used staff officers. Their role is primarily to keep the flow of papers and actions going whether or not the secretary (or general or admiral or air vice-marshal) has made the requested decision or signed the requested paper. They need to understand the issues under consideration, the likely line the secretary will take and the factors involved and know the likely time line for decisions. They take minutes of the executive meetings and may sit in on some other meetings to keep a record. They also have easy access to the secretary and can alert him or her to particular deadlines or concerns. They can also be a sounding board for the secretary on the mood of the organisation, or parts of the organisation.

Table 11.3 'Staffing' as a verb

A lesson from the Department of Defence was the use of the word 'staffing' as a verb, not a noun.

This use relates to the process before a matter is put to a senior defence committee or executive for a decision to ensure there has been adequate consultation and the outstanding differences narrowed sufficiently to allow efficient and effective use of senior management's time. The matter must be 'staffed'.

Staff officers in particular are expected to manage this process, not to limit options or force consensus, but to help senior management focus on the critical issues and options and to ensure managers down the line take and share responsibility rather than delegate upwards. The process is not, however, reliant on having staff officers—it can work through other means of horizontal management across programs and divisions ahead of senior management decision making.

The staff officer (or senior executive assistant) and the departmental secretary need to be careful. In the Defence department, I often saw staff officers overplay their hands and their two or three-star officer bosses found themselves pressed into a position without sufficient personal attention towards the issues and implications (sometimes the fault lay with a lazy senior officer). On occasions, the staff officers also exaggerated the power and authority of their general or admiral, distancing him from others rather than ensuring better communications.

Another danger that occurred once or twice in the Housing department was allowing the senior executive assistant to inhibit the vital relationship among the department's executive. I made the mistake of asking my senior executive assistant to sit in on some sensitive executive discussions and to take minutes, when those discussions needed to be in private: my deputies made their anger known to me very sharply afterwards!

As a rule, I was extremely well served by my senior executive assistants. I also used the position to help develop some promising executive-level staff who needed some 'broadening' before being considered for more senior jobs.

I did not use a staff officer in the APS Commission as the span of control did not warrant it. Besides, I had an executive assistant then who was more than capable of playing both roles.

The other element of personal support within the department is the relationship among the departmental executive. This relationship is essentially professional, but it is always personal too. This does not mean regular dinner parties at home, but a genuine empathy that provides support whether through difficult times in the department or challenges in personal lives. Attending the funeral of a colleague's close family member or celebrating a family wedding—these minor gestures strengthen ties and ensure broader mutual support.

The critical factor in the relationship is trust among all parties, notwithstanding the authority of the secretary.

Table 11.4 Trust within the executive

Tony Ayers taught me a key principle behind ensuring trust within a small executive when I joined him in the Department of Defence in 1990. At our first meeting on the first morning, he told me firmly that if I had a dispute with any of the other deputies under no circumstances was I to raise the matter privately with him. I was to sort it out myself directly or, if that was not possible, to raise the matter openly with the others present for a confidential but collegiate discussion.

I insisted on exactly the same behaviour in each agency I managed, and in every case the executive worked well, with trust and mutual personal support.

It is lonely at the top, and not even the deputies can be enjoined in some issues. Michael Keating took me out to lunch when I was first appointed secretary to give me some useful private advice. Perhaps the best element was his advice to maintain some external networks, particularly among other secretaries I respected highly, not only for advice on specific matters I could not discuss within the department (indeed often I could not discuss any specifics with anyone outside either), but for more general mutual support.

This I did, not only with some fellow secretaries but with longstanding friends and former colleagues, ensuring substantial support and also keeping my feet on the ground through continuing contacts with people with different perspectives on work and life. I consciously maintained about four or five networks, mostly in Canberra but also in Sydney and abroad.

Finally, but not least in importance, is the support of family. I never did get the balance right between work and family, but my weakness was made up by my family's tolerance and support. I am not sure that future secretaries can assume the same.

Performance assessment

As mentioned in Chapter 6, a key contributor to organisational performance is the timely, positive, comprehensive and fair feedback to individuals on their performance, along with clear alignment between their work requirements and the organisation's objectives. The agency head also needs regular feedback and confirmation that he or she is focusing on the right things.

The next chapter on the role of the Public Service Commissioner describes the processes that used to exist for assessing the performance of secretaries. I have also written elsewhere about the problems of performance pay for secretaries, particularly the risk of overemphasising political factors and under-emphasising professional management, leadership and the promotion of APS Values. I am pleased the Rudd Government has dropped performance pay for secretaries, but there is now the danger that feedback might also disappear.

Before performance pay, I used the department's strategic plan as a form of agreement with the minister going beyond the outputs and outcomes identified in budget documentation to cover a wide range of management priorities: in essence, a form of 'balanced score card'. It went beyond my personal responsibilities but, in the absence of a formal performance agreement, it provided a reasonable basis for feedback on my performance. I did not seek such feedback from the minister or the Secretary of the Department of PM&C (or the APS Commission) in any formal way, but I did try to speak to the minister a least once a year about how we were tracking against the plan, and more generally against his expectations.

With the introduction of performance pay, the process became more formalised. I generally prepared a short minute to the minister near the beginning of the year on the priorities I should personally address, drawing on the strategic plan and the Prime Minister's charter letter. I sought opportunities about twice a year for personal feedback and, in line with the formal processes, prepared a 'self-evaluation' each year for the minister's endorsement before passing it on to the Secretary of the Department of PM&C and the APS Commission.

Mostly, the feedback discussions with the minister were only tangentially related to the minute I had originally prepared or the self-evaluation.

Table 11.5 Ministerial feedback

The aide-mémoire I prepared for the minister in 2000 regarding my performance agreement for the year listed:

- specific policy and program priorities
- specific management priorities
- ministerial support activities
- leadership priorities
- values issues (highlighting accountability, managing conflicts of interest and promoting public service professionalism).

The discussion I had with Minister Wooldridge in December 2000 in fact canvassed informally a wider range of related matters, including:

- my personal style, including whether (as Moore-Wilton had advocated) I should spend more time in the minister's office (the minister confirmed his preference for my practice of working mostly from the department)
- my policy advising, including the priorities for my personal attention (the minister was particularly keen for me to remain closely involved in all budget matters)
- a number of management issues, primarily concerning the quality of the top team and succession management (the minister was mostly highly complimentary about the team) but also about resource pressures on the department and my proposal to involve an external person on the department's management committee (he supported Bill Scales' involvement)
- some leadership issues (the minister was keen for me to maintain and strengthen links with various health professional organisations and complimented me on the role I played across the portfolio) and communications management (the minister wanted me to give this more attention, particularly the capacity to respond quickly to media criticisms of the government, which I struggled to do)
- appointments to portfolio boards
- Centenary of Federation celebrations, including the eightieth anniversary of the first Commonwealth Department of Health.

Subsequent to this discussion, I provided the minister with notes against the agreed priorities set out in the original aide-mémoire, taking into account his comments. My notes highlighted:

- on policy and program priorities, the private health insurance Lifetime Community Cover success, the progress on rural initiatives and the progress on health reform initiatives such as health information, enhanced primary care through the MOU with GPs and other agreements that also improved financial risk management
- on management, the lessons drawn from the aged care and MRI crises and the turnaround in both areas in terms of quality and financial control, the strengthening of the department's senior team and the competent management of IT outsourcing
- on ministerial support, the improvement in managing communications and correspondence while noting there was further to go
- on leadership, the improved governance arrangements in the department and portfolio and my personal role in strengthening linkages across the health system and promoting a coherent strategic direction
- on values, highlighting my standing with the IPAA and our improvements in managing conflicts of interest since the MRI crisis.

The minister endorsed my notes, which I then copied to Moore-Wilton and Williams for consideration in their advice to the Prime Minister on my performance. The performance pay suspended in 2000 was reinstated in 2001 and I was also reappointed to the Health department on a new three-year contract.

I also looked for an opportunity each year, before finalising the annual report, to seek feedback on how well the department had performed in meeting the minister's requirements in each program area. From this, we were able to prepare the assessment in the published report but, as well, the discussion inevitably provided feedback on my own performance and that of my senior staff from the point of view of the minister.

The Secretary of the Department of PM&C provided occasional feedback, also which, while usually negative in Moore-Wilton's case and not particularly welcome, was probably better than not getting any at all. I wrote to Moore-Wilton twice responding to his comments (in addition to providing the 'self-evaluation' agreed by the minister), but he did not reply either orally or in writing.

The Public Service Commissioner, Helen Williams, provided background to the assessments being made and offered helpful advice from time to time on how best to respond to criticisms being made. Like me, however, she was not a favourite of Moore-Wilton, and she did not share his assessments of me.

During the MRI and 'kerosene baths' crises, I was also constantly warned that my future was under threat.

Table 11.6 Other performance feedback or scapegoating

The 'kerosene baths' crisis was the most harrowing of personal experiences, it being made clear on a number of occasions between March and June 2000 that my own position was under threat.

Formally, of course, I could expect my performance appraisal for 1999–2000 to include consideration of the MRI and aged-care incidents in the assessment of how well I had managed the department and supported ministers. I had no doubt my performance would be rated poorly if for no other reason than that the political damage would demand that the department (and I) should carry much of the responsibility. This was not entirely fair in my view, but an inevitable result of the political framework governing the performance assessment process. I was prepared therefore for being denied any performance pay.

More worryingly, however, were the informal assessments and scuttlebutt among people with no relevant competence but considerable political influence. I mentioned earlier (Table 3.7) the advice from a key member of the PMO that 'you need a baseball bat, Andrew, to take to the department'. This was clearly an indication that some ministerial staff wanted to weigh into me too. A senior member of Wooldridge's staff warned me directly that my position was being discussed among ministerial staff, and possibly ministers, and that termination of my appointment was seriously under consideration. I responded that this was quite inappropriate and, in any case, action against me would not relieve pressure on ministers, particularly Minister Bishop. I spoke to Helen Williams, Public Service Commissioner, and decided firmly I would not resign. She kindly ensured I had information about superannuation options should I suddenly be sacked.

I also received advice in March 2000 from a senior officer in the Department of PM&C that the social policy area of that department was strongly criticising me and the department, including in communications with the PMO. This, I was told, reflected a common approach taken by that area of PM&C at the time, to work directly not only with the PMO but other ministers' offices and to infer that it could handle program management as well as policy advising better than the relevant line departments (these included education and immigration as well as health

---

and aged care). It was an approach others in the Department of PM&C considered inconsistent with the department's coordination role and inappropriate because it encouraged ministerial staff to contribute to matters outside their competence.

I continued as Secretary of the Health department for nearly two years after this, with my contract renewed in 2001 after Wooldridge confirmed his support for my reappointment (see Table 11.5). On his departure after the 2001 election, however, I was replaced as secretary and became Public Service Commissioner.

Changes since the 1980s

The processes of career development of secretaries have been changing with greater mobility particularly at the SES level, and with more external appointments of agency heads. While the majority of secretaries are still people with a long career in the APS, there is an increasing proportion with other lengthy experience, whether in state public services or in private or non-governmental organisations (mostly with close involvement with government). This trend is widening the background, perspectives and skill sets of secretaries.

At the same time, as mentioned in Chapter 2, the trend since the 1980s to require secretaries to be both managers and policy advisers has perhaps led to some convergence of styles and skills. There seem to be fewer mavericks or characters with highly specialist skills or individual styles (whether an Ian Castles or a Pat Lanigan—the enigmatic Director-General of Social Security in the late 1970s). Everyone is expected to be a manager today, perhaps at the cost of fewer top policy analysts among the secretaries' group.

Issues arising

A perennial issue is the balance between generalists and specialists, or each secretary's own balance between generalist and specialist skills and knowledge. There is a need for a mix among the cadre of secretaries and agency heads, but also there are risks for a secretary who is either too specialist (and lacking broad management skills or deep understanding of the processes of government and political awareness) or too generalist (and lacking essential subject content).

The increase in mobility adds weight to the Australian practice of more laissez faire approaches to career development. There is, however, a strong case for strengthening the investment in future leaders given the pressures on secretaries and the responsibilities they exercise. This requires careful succession management to identify those who should receive such investments. And it suggests that those who come in laterally to secretary or other very senior positions need to have access to substantial formal and informal support.

The increase in mobility should not, however, be exaggerated. The current leadership is still dominated by individuals who joined the APS or a state public service on or shortly after graduation. That might remain the case. If so, it also remains essential that the Public Service recruits some of the best and brightest from our universities and convinces them to stay.

Successful development almost always involves on-the-job experience. Formal training, however, is increasingly important, providing a framework for applying lessons from experience to new situations and for analysing the causes of success and failure. There are serious risks, however, in the fads and fashions of management theories and training, including wasted resources on overheads and on unnecessary restructuring together with loss of credibility among staff within the agency and external stakeholders.

I believe performance pay for secretaries shifted the balance of incentives too far towards rewarding responsiveness and away from rewarding good management, leadership and the promotion of public service professionalism. There is a risk, however, in removing performance pay that feedback to secretaries will also disappear. Secretaries, like other employees, require constructive, fair, comprehensive and timely feedback on their performance. There might be an opportunity now to introduce a performance assessment process that relies more on peer review, as in Canada or New Zealand, with ministerial feedback included but not dominating. Reports could still go to the Prime Minister for noting and comments (see Chapter 12).

Lessons learned

I am acutely conscious that my career experience, while personally very rewarding, should not be seen as the model for others to try to replicate. It is my personal history, reflecting my choices, my good fortune and my own strengths and weaknesses.

What capabilities and experiences do secretaries require? I do not suggest there is a simple formula. Indeed, there is advantage to the Public Service as a whole to have a diversity of people at the top with different personalities, skill mixes, expertise and personal and career backgrounds. Nonetheless, those trying to guide career development rightly look for some balance in the mix of each secretary's experience, seeing benefits in:

* some management experience and some formal management training
* policy capacity, which remains critical for most Commonwealth departments
* some central agency experience as well as line agency experience
* some proven expertise, even if the person is now in a more generalist role.

The last is, in my view, quite important. In some cases, there remains a need for the relevant secretary to have particular subject matter expertise (for example, in the Attorney-General's Department and in Treasury). In others, the secretary might not require subject matter expertise, but must appreciate its importance to the success of the department. I was always persuaded by a comment Sir John Crawford made to a forum at The Australian National University that I attended in 1970 to the effect that the best generalist was someone who had been an expert. I also tend to favour some streaming of most top people according to areas of expertise, despite my own eclectic career. That streaming might reflect expertise in social policy, or industry, or defence and foreign affairs, or economics and financial management, or law, or large-scale management.

Whatever our own attributes, secretaries require substantial support in terms of personal staff, the agency's executive team and external networks. Cementing personal commitment and trust is essential and there are some simple rules to follow that can help.

I have highlighted the importance of retaining some form of performance feedback, primarily peer based, despite the welcome removal of performance pay. The five areas identified under the old regime remain apposite: support for the minister, support for the government as a whole, management, leadership and the APS Values. In saying this, I should also caution against too much formality in the process. With this in mind, I encourage readers to examine a Canadian paper, *Distinguishing the real from the surreal in management reform*, by two former deputy ministers (the Canadian equivalent of Australian departmental secretaries), Ian Clark and Harry Swain (2007), in which they distinguish between the duties of deputy ministers to manage people and public monies in a sensible way and duties to comply with centrally imposed requirements associated with idealised government-wide management frameworks.

12. Inside or outside the tent: the role of the Public Service Commissioner

I was Public Service Commissioner for three years from the beginning of 2002 until the end of 2004. The position is a statutory office under the *Public Service Act 1999* and, once appointed, a commissioner cannot be removed other than by the Parliament. The commissioner nonetheless has a minister (in fact, two: the Prime Minister and the Minister Assisting the Prime Minister on the Public Service).

The following summarises the role from my experience, using similar headings to those of the earlier chapters concerning departmental secretaries, which can be used to summarise the responsibilities of almost all heads of government agencies. The differences in the commissioner's role are reflected in the very different amounts of time spent on the various responsibilities of an agency head.

Table 12.1 Time allocation by secretary and commissioner

Area of activity	Departmental secretary (%)	Public Service Commissioner (%)
(a) Supporting the minister	35–50	< 10
(b) Supporting the government as a whole	< 5	< 5
(c) Working with the Parliament	up to 5 +	5–10
(d) Management of the department/agency	15–30	15–20
(e) Management of the portfolio	up to 5	nil
(f) External relationships — with other Commonwealth agencies	5	15
— with other governments	10	< 5
— with non-governmental bodies	5–10	< 5
(g) Contributing to APS capability	up to 5	50

Again, a number of activities could be allocated to several headings. Time spent on APS Commission and MAC reports and on commission events and programs as commissioner has been allocated here to 'contributing to APS capability', while 'supporting the government as a whole' relates mostly to involvement in portfolio secretaries' meetings and related activities not initiated by the commission.

The extra time involved in working with the Parliament was because I was also the Parliamentary Service Commissioner. Since the latter position was created in 1999, the presiding officers have asked the Public Service Commissioner to take the role.

Promoting the APS Values and contributing to APS capability

As these are at the centre of the commissioner's statutory responsibilities, I will describe them first rather than last.

The main elements of this work as commissioner are:

- issuing directions and developing and disseminating guidelines on the APS Values and Code of Conduct
- developing and supporting the leadership cadre of the APS (SES and agency heads)
- working through the MAC to identify good management practice in areas of shared interest across the APS
- evaluating and reporting on how agencies are upholding the APS Values
- succession management and agency head performance assessment.

Guidelines

When I was appointed commissioner, my predecessor, Helen Williams, had issued the directions required under the new legislation on the APS Values and Code of Conduct. These, appropriately in my view, clarified the responsibilities of agency heads while leaving them some room to manage how they would promote the values and ensure the code was upheld. My focus was on developing guidelines to help agency heads and their employees to apply the values and Code of Conduct in their practical work situations.

My earlier, practical experience as a departmental secretary made me somewhat sceptical of some of the rhetoric of the management literature and the fads and fashions involved in management theory. I therefore put considerable emphasis on what I called 'hardwiring', whether of the APS Values or of the concept of leadership, both of which were emphasised in the *Public Service Act 1999*.

So, for example, I grouped the 15 values in the act under four headings, which identified public servants' key relationships and behaviours, and clarified how the values reflected the unique role of the Public Service under the Westminster system (for example, responsive to the elected government, non-partisan, impartial, merit based). This grouping of the values guided the structure of the *State of the Service Reports* from 2002 and the rewriting of the Guidelines on Official Conduct in 2003. Using OECD experience, we also identified how agency heads could go about 'embedding' the values in their organisations in practical ways through 'commitment', 'management' and 'assurance' activities. This led to the following diagram (Figure 12.1) to illustrate the practical approach we were advocating and the guidelines we prepared for agency heads on embedding the values in their organisations.

Figure 12.1 The APS Values framework

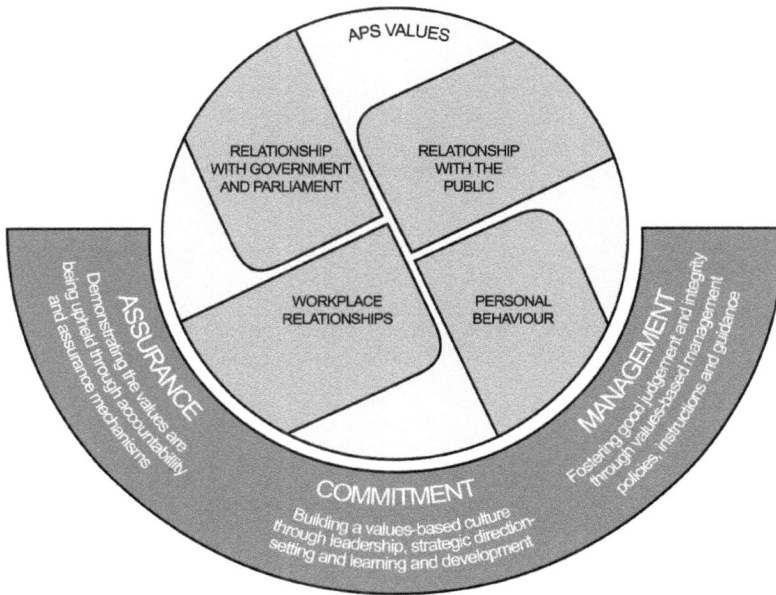

This work recognised the different business responsibilities of agencies and how these might reflect differences in priorities among the APS Values (for example, Centrelink might give more weight to values concerning the relationship its staff have with the public while the Department of PM&C might give more weight to values concerning the relationship its staff has with the government and the Parliament), but confirmed the unifying role and relevance of the full set of APS Values.

Leadership development

Similarly, I was becoming uneasy about the language of 'leadership'. The SES Leadership Capability Framework had proven to be very robust, with richness in its detail and language, but there was a push to apply the framework to everyone at every level. I felt this ran the danger of making it meaningless. We therefore did some extensive research into the skills and attributes that were really required at different levels, recognising that there could be wide disparities for different jobs in different businesses. I was also concerned not to understate the importance of technical expertise or the specific skills required of managers at different levels. The ensuing Integrated Leadership System (ILS), released in 2004, gained considerable credibility throughout the Public Service precisely because of this practical balance, as illustrated by Figure 12.2, which appeared near the beginning of the ILS documentation.

Figure 12.2 The changing mix of skills and capabilities

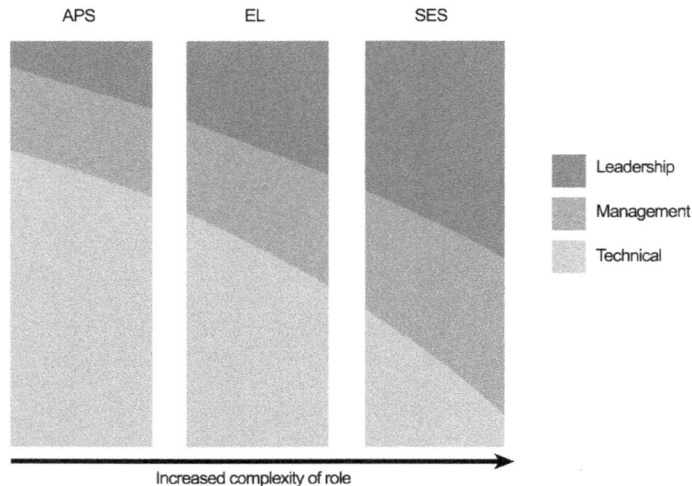

The ILS led to a substantial refreshment of our suite of APS Commission development programs, though these continued to focus mostly on the SES and the feeder groups into the SES.

My personal involvement in these was extensive, both in the design and in their delivery. I attended all the courses for new SES officers, which were held three or four times a year, to discuss the statutory obligations of SES officers in promoting and upholding the APS Values and in working throughout the APS—not just within their own agencies. Often I would raise common ethical dilemmas and encourage discussion of how they might be handled. I also attended many of the other leadership programs managed by the commission or run by agencies for their own staff.

A particularly useful program was the Career Assessment Centre for staff at EL2 level considered likely to be promoted to the SES in the future. The value of this program for those participating and their agencies was in its direct assessment, without pulling punches. An added value for the commission was the capacity to collate the assessments and to build a picture of common strengths and weaknesses and trends over time, to help in the design of future development activities. This analysis showed that most of these high-flying staffers were skilled in communication and demonstrated personal commitment and integrity, but many were weak in shaping strategic thinking and maintaining productive working relations.

The Management Advisory Committee

Our APS Commission guidelines were prepared through an extensive process of consultation with agencies, mostly using a reference group of secretaries and drawing on APS-wide case studies. MAC reports similarly used reference groups and case studies, but also employed a team of deputy secretaries to pull the material together. This had the added virtue of allowing secretaries to see close at hand deputy secretaries from other agencies who might be candidates for advancement in the future, thus contributing to succession management.

I was always closely involved in the MAC projects as the commissioner was the 'executive officer' of the MAC under the *Public Service Act*. I initiated some projects, prepared papers for the MAC on the scope of each one and was on every reference group of secretaries.

Those that I contributed most to were the 2002 report *Organisational Renewal*, on the likely demographic impact on the APS and the need for improved workforce planning, and the 2004 report *Connected Government*, on the management of whole-of-government policies and projects. I had previously contributed substantially to the 2001 report *Performance Management in the APS: A strategic framework*.

Table 12.2 Connected Government: improving whole-of-government capacity

Peter Shergold, Secretary of the Department of PM&C, initiated the 2004 MAC review of whole-of-government management, with strong support from me as Public Service Commissioner.

Roger Beale (Environment department) chaired the reference group of secretaries and agency heads and Lisa Paul (later Secretary of Education) led the deputy secretary project team; Lynne Tacy (Deputy Public Service Commissioner) provided the most substantial contribution among the deputies' group.

The project drew on a wide range of case studies of whole-of-government exercises, including the response to the Bali bombings, the management of the Sydney Olympics, the establishment and role of the Australian Greenhouse Office, the COAG Indigenous trials, the Goodna service integration project, the National Illicit Drugs Strategy and *iconsult* (a proposed electronic information exchange on community consultations).

The final report canvassed:

- the most appropriate structures and processes for managing whole-of-government matters (Beale contributed most to this chapter)
- cultural aspects that might facilitate cooperation and collaboration (Tacy and the APS Commission contributed most to this)

- information management and infrastructure (with particular help from Helen Williams from the Department of Communications, Information Technology and the Arts)
- budget and accountability framework (assisted by the Finance department, with considerable cajoling from line department secretaries and me)
- engagement beyond the APS (I contributed substantially to this chapter, along with the heads of several service delivery agencies)
- crisis management (DFAT contributed substantially to this chapter, along with Paul, who had played a key role in the Bali bombings response).

I believe the report has had a significant impact on APS practice, improving capability through shared learning. For example, crisis management is now a well-drilled process throughout the Commonwealth and there is more careful consideration of the structures and processes appropriate for different types of problems than in the past. This body of work also influenced the subsequent development of the Cabinet Implementation Unit.

State of the Service Reports

The main avenue for evaluating and reporting on how agencies are upholding the values is the commissioner's yearly *State of the Service Report*. Helen Williams prepared the first two reports required under the legislation, developing an initial framework and infrastructure including a detailed survey of agencies. I built on this using the grouping of the APS Values I had proposed to clarify the main areas of performance I wished to focus on (relations with ministers and the government, relations with the public, workplace relations and personal behaviour) and adding a weighted random sample survey of APS employees to complement (and test) the survey of agencies.

Together with the commission's own database, which tracked all APS employees, this provided an increasingly comprehensive evidence base to support judgments on performance against the APS Values and on APS capability. In my last report in 2004, I also introduced some information on the views of the public collected by some agencies through their own feedback mechanisms.

The surveys covered sensitive issues such as relations between public servants and ministers and their advisers, and public servants' confidence in upholding the APS Values in this area. The data were fascinating, but caused considerable angst among my colleagues.

Table 12.3 Washing hands: handling sensitive data

The initial APS employee survey included questions on relations with ministers and their officers, whether the employees had had direct contact in the previous 12 months, whether they had faced challenges in upholding the APS Values in these contacts and their confidence in handling challenges.

Peter Shergold, Secretary of the Department of PM&C, asked me to brief portfolio secretaries in advance on the data collected for the *State of the Service Report*. I put together some raw tables that I had not yet fully analysed and about which I had yet to draft any commentary.

I distributed the tables at a meeting of portfolio secretaries highlighting what I felt were the most significant results, including that an amazingly high 26 per cent of all employees (including staff at all levels in all APS agencies including the Tax Office, Centrelink, Customs, the Bureau of Statistics, as well as ministerial departments) said they had had direct contact with the minister or minister's office and that many had faced challenges in upholding the values, though most were confident they could manage them.

There was at first disbelief and then, when I stood by the validity of the data, unease about what it meant and what should be done with it. The data confirmed the growing importance of ministerial staff and the extent of their reach into the Public Service—a matter of some political sensitivity at the time. One secretary said, 'If we are not sure what it means, why are we publishing it?', to which I responded that '"we" are not publishing it, I am'.

Shergold's nervousness, and that of most present, led him to propose that all copies of the data be returned to me there and then so that it was clearly the commissioner's responsibility to analyse and report on it; secretaries then would not feel under any obligation to advise their ministers of the sensitive information until I reported. I was therefore given back all the tables and, somewhat bemused, returned to the commission to continue my analysis and start drafting the report.

While the quality of the reports, and of their underpinning data and analysis, was improving, I was nonetheless cautious about identifying the agencies whose performance was weak. I felt I needed to build our reputation for credible analysis before taking the step of 'naming and shaming'. Instead, I named examples of good practice and provided agency heads with data on their agencies compared with the overall data so they could see where they were or were not performing well and consider whether action was needed to address weaknesses.

Succession management

The commissioner has no statutory role in the appointment of secretaries and agency heads, other than in the case of the Secretary of the Department of PM&C. I did, however, contribute to succession management by the Secretary of PM&C by providing a database on potential candidates and on each agency head position (extending the process developed by Williams). The data were based largely on interviews I held each year with secretaries about their deputies and equivalent, and about other SES officers seen as 'high fliers', and data the secretaries subsequently provided on their experience and strengths and suggestions for future development. I also encouraged confidential discussion at the portfolio secretaries' retreats of the capabilities of deputies and equivalent under protocols that required firsthand evidence to support any view expressed. These discussions were critical, as they facilitated moderation of the claims of each secretary about his or her own staff (and they did reveal some very different assessments of some staff). As commissioner, I generally added my own comments to the information base held in the commission, drawing in part on these conversations.

Secretaries quite often contacted me for suggestions about people they might encourage to apply for senior vacancies, accepting that my advice would reflect my interests in broader capability building throughout the Public Service and not only my views on likely strong candidates for the specific vacancies concerned.

Occasionally, the Secretary of the Department of PM&C and the commissioner took a highly proactive stance on succession management, setting up a committee of secretaries to advise on possible rotations of deputies to help their development. This did not happen while I was commissioner and earlier exercises had mixed success, with secretaries suspicious that individuals offered for transfer might not be high-performing ones and that those secretaries pursuing others' deputies might be motivated by self-interest rather than the broader interests of the APS.

Performance assessment

Once a year, much of my time was taken up with managing the process of performance assessment of departmental secretaries and executive agency heads. This related to the Howard Government's arrangements for performance pay, which I am pleased the Rudd Government has dispensed with. I have described the process in some detail elsewhere.[1] With some modification (including the removal of bonus payments), the process would still be worthwhile in my view.

In summary, secretaries would prepare self-assessments and discuss these with their ministers. They would then forward these to the Secretary of the Department of PM&C and to me. The two of us would subsequently meet the portfolio ministers and seek comments on the assessments and views on overall performance. I then drafted a short report on each secretary for the Prime Minister, which the PM&C Secretary would consider before a final agreed version went to the Prime Minister. I often checked some of the supporting material, for example, by examining Auditor-General reports during this process. The final reports summarised our views against the suggested criteria (support for the minister, supporting the government as a whole, management, leadership, upholding the APS Values and implementation of government decisions) and the ministers' and our own recommended assessments. The two of us then met the Prime Minister to discuss the reports (after my meeting the Prime Minister on my own to discuss the performance of the Secretary of the Department of PM&C) and I would write to each secretary advising of the Prime Minister's decision.

I also managed the process of assessing the CEOs of executive agencies who were covered by performance pay. In their case, I handled most of the process on my own, seeking the endorsement of the Secretary of the Department of PM&C only at a late stage; the Prime Minister usually wanted only my assurance that the assessments were consistently applied and that the ministers concerned were in broad agreement (he usually accepted my advice to moderate some excessively generous ministerial assessments). My process in these cases included discussion with the relevant portfolio secretary as well as the minister most involved (generally not the portfolio minister).

Despite my strong criticisms of the overall process, it had some strengths that should be preserved in future performance feedback processes for secretaries:

- the suggested criteria were sensible, as long as they were all properly considered and balanced
- a self-assessment based on some agreement with the minister at the beginning of the year and then discussed with the minister at the end provided some structure to the process
- the Secretary of the Department of PM&C and the commissioner both checking with the ministers, and later both talking to the Prime Minister, ensured there was involvement of the operational and professional heads of the APS.

The changes I would like to see are:

- a stronger peer review element, where at least one other secretary (or perhaps a former secretary) participates in the process, making a more careful judgment of the management, leadership and APS Values criteria as well as reviewing the ministers' assessments
- the Prime Minister being asked more to endorse (or not) rather than decide on the performance assessment

- the performance assessment distinguishing only between strong performance, fully competent and not fully competent (the last giving notice that improvement is required).

Such an approach would line up more closely with the Canadian process; the New Zealand arrangement (where the State Services Commissioner is the employer of the secretaries) is even more independent of the political process.

Working with ministers

Governments have policies on public service management and the APS Commission advises ministers on these policies, seeks clarification of the policies and consults ministers on the commission's strategies and programs to ensure consistency with the government's policies. In this sense, the commissioner's role has similarity to that of a departmental secretary. The ministers concerned, however, have other portfolio responsibilities, which greatly overshadow those concerning the commission. The Prime Minister has very limited time to spend on public service matters and the minister assisting in my time was also Minister for Employment and Workplace Relations (under the Rudd Government, he is the ministerial Cabinet Secretary as well as Special Minister of State within the finance portfolio).

I sought monthly meetings with the minister assisting, partly to remind him we were there and to ensure a level of comfort with what we were doing. I was conscious of the risk of others displacing the commissioner as the key adviser on public service matters, including in particular the secretary of the minister's department. I also encouraged the minister assisting (without success) to have an adviser with clear responsibilities for public service matters, who was not just the department's liaison officer (DLO). It was not possible to justify a full-time officer to be a dedicated DLO for the commission, though I also tried to have the minister's chief of staff consider one of my people to play the shared role with the department. To be fair, the department's DLO generally played the liaison role with the commission quite effectively, but I still felt it was not the optimal solution for us.

Table 12.4 Advising on workplace relations within the APS

The APS Commission did not have responsibility for industrial relations matters in my time: that was the responsibility of the Employment and Workplace Relations department. Nonetheless, I did have statutory responsibilities to explain and promote the APS Values, which included a number relevant to industrial relations (for example, the merit principle, fairness, managing performance, consultations), and to develop APS employment policies and practices and facilitate continuous improvement.

When the minister, Tony Abbott, was pressing for all public servants to be on individual AWAs, I was concerned that his department was encouraging him without adequate advice on the issues and the problems involved. I became aware that the department had received legal advice that it would be possible to require all new appointees to the APS to be on AWAs, though not to require current employees to do so or to apply this as a condition for promotion. While this advice on the law might have been technically correct, it did not include consideration of the broader issues involved in any attempt to push for universal use of AWAs and I was not amused that it was sought and given without consultation with me (as required by standing rules on legal advice from the Attorney-General's Department).

I advised the minister of my statutory role to evaluate the extent to which agencies incorporated and upheld the values and that wider use of AWAs would require agencies to satisfy me that they were meeting the requirement of the merit principle. In my view, they would need clear, public remuneration policies, consistent with classification principles, and to demonstrate that open competition for promotion was not being circumvented by individually negotiated pay deals.

I also advised that organisational performance was not necessarily enhanced by individual-based pay flexibility even if this enhanced individual performance (and it was not clear if it did). More important elements include alignment with the organisation's objectives; timely, positive and fair feedback; and management addressing obstacles to individual and team performance.

Finally, I drew to his attention the views of the CEOs of every large APS agency (including the Tax Office, Centrelink, Customs and the Bureau of Statistics) that the administrative workload to manage individual AWAs for all staff would be excessive.

The minister said he appreciated my advice, but it was clear he was more appreciative of the advice I believe he received from the secretary of his department.

I generally only met the Prime Minister each year when advising on agency heads' performance and at joint forums such as the portfolio secretaries' retreat. While my written communications were usually with the minister assisting, I did send the Prime Minister some minutes directly, particularly on highly significant issues (for example, after the 2004 election, I advised him on a range of public administration matters for the next term of government including ministerial advisers' code of conduct and secretaries' contracts and performance pay).

Whole-of-government work

The commissioner is involved in many forums of secretaries, not only those focused on the APS management matters described above. This serves two purposes:

- it ensures the commissioner is fully aware of the challenges facing agencies, and can help to ensure the APS Commission work is relevant and helpful
- the commissioner is usually an experienced senior public servant sometimes able to contribute to discussions on particular policies, programs and processes other than through the prisms of the responsible agency heads. I certainly contributed my views on such matters as population ageing, Indigenous welfare and Commonwealth–state relations, for example.

Working with the Parliament

My interaction with the Parliament related to both my statutory responsibilities: as Public Service Commissioner and as Parliamentary Service Commissioner. The two roles are quite distinct and it is only by convention that the Public Service Commissioner is invited by the presiding officers (the Speaker of the House of Representatives and the President of the Senate) to be the Parliamentary Service Commissioner, a role created by the *Parliamentary Service Act 1999*.

Public Service Commissioner and the Parliament

My interaction with the Parliament as Public Service Commissioner was more limited than it had been as a departmental secretary. I suspect this is because there are fewer sensitive political issues involved for Members of Parliament to pursue.

The APS Commission was always listed on the agenda for Senate Estimates, but I think we were only once asked to appear during my time as Public Service Commissioner.

This surprised me given the opportunity my *State of the Service Report* presented for senators to explore my views of the performance of individual agencies as well as the APS as a whole, and the degree to which the APS Values were being upheld under the Howard Government. Notwithstanding increasing media interest in the reports, as we introduced a survey of employees that contained such sensitive issues as relations with ministers and their offices, I was never asked questions on my reports by the Parliament.

I was asked to contribute to the Senate Committee inquiries into a Certain Maritime Incident ('Children overboard') and ministerial staff. I took the opportunity in these to argue in favour of a code of conduct for ministerial staff as part of a process to improve their professionalism given their increasingly important role. In contrast with my earlier experience as a departmental secretary appearing before Senate Committees, these times I was treated far more as a professional expert rather than as a manager of government programs or an adviser on government policies.

Parliamentary Service Commissioner's role

My role as Parliamentary Service Commissioner was initially low-key. I established regular meetings of the heads of the parliamentary departments to discuss matters of common interest relating to people management and the Parliamentary Service Values (which differed in important respects to the APS Values given the independence of the Parliamentary Service from the executive arm of government). We canvassed ways in which the parliamentary departments might adapt some of the public service developments led by the APS Commission in areas such as leadership development, embedding values, workforce planning and performance management. I also prepared a very short annual report describing developments in the Parliamentary Service.

In 2003, however, the presiding officers asked me to conduct a review of the administration of the Parliament—an exercise that required much more of my time. I engaged a consultant with financial management experience to assist me and also drew on some resources within the APS Commission. I was pleased that the review led to a major restructuring of the departments, after many decades of failed attempts to do so.

Table 12.5 Parliamentary Service Commissioner's review of the administration of the Parliament

In 2003, the President of the Senate and Speaker of the House formally requested that I review the administration of the Parliament. They were concerned generally about government criticism of the costs involved and the need to demonstrate to the government that they had fully considered opportunities for improvements in efficiency, and they were specifically concerned that security arrangements had not been reviewed since 11 September 2001.

Given the APS Commission's lack of expertise in financial management, I engaged a former senior finance official, Len Early, to work with me and my corporate manager, Mike Jones, on the review. We worked in close consultation with the three heads of the five parliamentary departments (one headed the three departments serving both houses) and their offices; we also consulted the Finance department but carefully maintained our independence from it. With advice from security agencies, I presented an initial report on security, recommending centralisation of security services and a strategic reassessment (almost certainly requiring additional funds), with a 'common services' model where the

---

different parliamentary departments would purchase services from a central provider.

In discussion with the two presiding officers, I indicated that the common services model might not be the optimal solution for the overall administration of the Parliament, and they invited me to look more broadly in my final report. I was very conscious, however, that the alternative of a rationalisation of the five departments had been debated and rejected many times during the previous 100 years and was passionately opposed by some, including the Clerk of the Senate.

Accordingly, I asked the commission's librarian, Jill Adams, to prepare a research paper reviewing the history of these debates and the arguments involved. This paper proved to be the critical element of the review: it identified the two major issues as the separation of the legislature from the Executive and bicameralism. If my recommendations could satisfactorily address these concerns, the option of rationalising the departments was feasible.

I noted in my final report the provisions in the new *Parliamentary Service Act 1999* that protected the independence of the legislature and the independence of the two clerks. I recommended a move to three departments (previous reviews had mostly proposed one or two departments), thereby not threatening bicameralism through the continued operation of separate departments for each house. I also recommended a somewhat independent Parliamentary Librarian within the (combined) Parliamentary Services department, thereby ensuring a considerable degree of independence in the support given to Members of Parliament.

The presiding officers firmly supported my recommendations, but the Clerk of the Senate campaigned strongly against them. The Senate eventually accepted my recommendations on condition of some further strengthening of the role of the Parliamentary Librarian, and both houses agreed to the proposed changes.

Management of the commission

The commission was far smaller than the departments I managed and I used a more streamlined approach to structures and plans, and was able to work in direct contact with most staff.

APSC Executive team in 2004: Lynne Tacy, Andrew Podger and Jeff Lamond (with Podger's favourite Garry Shead painting) (photo by kind permission of the Australian Public Service Commission)

Nonetheless, I still found strategic planning very useful. In the initial planning when I arrived in 2002, we agreed it was important to build on Helen Williams' achievements in implementing the new *Public Service Act 1999*, looking to take advantage of its provisions to enhance the role and contribution of the commission in enhancing the performance and capability of the APS. Our approach relied heavily on strengthening relations with APS agencies, which in turn relied on our credibility and expertise. Later on, we revised the plan to take advantage of Peter Shergold's appointment as Secretary of the Department of PM&C and his interest in reinvigorating the MAC.

Among the developments foreshadowed in our plans that we successfully pursued during my time as commissioner were:

*   major guides on the APS Values and Code of Conduct
*   strengthening of the *State of the Service Report* with the introduction of a sample survey of employees, allowing more robust and independent evaluation
*   new MAC reports including on organisational renewal and connected government

- the extension of the SES leadership capability framework into the broader Integrated Leadership System and refocusing the commission's leadership and management development activities.

Part of this success was due to strengthening what was already a pretty good team in the commission. When Jeff Lamond became the Merit Protection Commissioner, we had a strong and united executive team (Lamond, Lynne Tacy and myself). We were also fortunate to recruit several excellent analysts from the Department of Employment and Workplace Relations (DEWR), who were pleased to transfer away from an environment they felt was not supportive of traditional APS values, and who complemented the expertise we already had in human resources and in decision review processes. I also recruited a rather flamboyant but highly skilled human resources expert from the Queensland Government. While not every appointment I made was successful, I was able to pass a very strong team on to my successor.

One aspect of agency management that was very different in the commission was its reliance on non-appropriation revenue. Just less than half of the commission's revenue comes from the services it provides on a user-pays basis. These include training and development programs and assistance to agencies in managing staff selection processes. Such revenue is not guaranteed: the commission must earn it on the basis of the quality of its services. A significant part of this revenue-raising activity is undertaken in the commission's state offices, working where most APS staff are located: outside Canberra. The offices in Western Australia, South Australia and Victoria were particularly successful, not only in serving APS staff but in linking with state government agencies and partnering with the IPAA. In most states, the APS Commission hosted the Regional Directors' Forums of APS agencies.

While this market discipline helps the commission to ensure the relevance and quality of its work, the risks involved constrain management's capacity to employ continuing staff and they also require smart investment in developing new and relevant products and services. We did not always do this well, but I was grateful to Ian Watt, Secretary of the Department of Finance, who agreed to a capital injection to allow us to review our leadership development strategy and introduce a new and revised set of products. In the event, this proved highly successful.

External relations

In the commission, many statutory responsibilities involve working with other APS agencies. The most time consuming is certifying the processes for SES appointments or promotion. While much of the workload involved was carried out by the commissioner's representative (usually an SES officer from another agency) on the relevant selection committee and by the deputy commissioner, agency heads frequently rang me to discuss who might be my representative and potential candidates for transfer or promotion; later, they might telephone to give me advance information on who they were likely to be appointing to the job. In the event of a potential problem over my certifying a selection process, there was certainly extensive discussion.

Table 12.6 Protecting the merit principle

My representative on an SES selection committee, and the secretary concerned, contacted me when a minister made it clear that he would not work with the preferred candidate for a deputy secretary position. My representative stated firmly that the preferred candidate had clearly won the job on merit and the second-ranked candidate fell well behind. The secretary agreed. The minister's objections were not based on close knowledge of the individual, but on an unwillingness to have someone from an academic institution that had publicly provided expert advice to the then Opposition.

I provided the secretary with my advice by email. The person concerned was not partisan and had won the job on merit. I would not certify the current process if it led to a candidate being appointed other than the currently preferred one. The job could be readvertised, but if the currently preferred candidate applied, I would only certify a process recommending someone else if, on merit, that person was clearly better.

The secretary spoke to the person concerned, noting the minister's attitude.

The person decided not to apply when the job was readvertised.

I sent a minute to my minister on the matter noting that, while the relevant minister had not contravened the *Public Service Act* by giving the secretary a direction, he had broken the spirit of the legislation and the merit principle by indicating refusal to work with the person selected on merit. The person affected would have been an excellent choice and, in time, I have no doubt he would have worked well with the minister. I also advised my intention to refer to the matter in the *State of the Service Report*, but without mentioning the department as this could lead to a breach of privacy.

The reference in the *State of the Service Report* was evidently too oblique, as it attracted no public or parliamentary interest.

Other statutory responsibilities include whistleblower cases and investigating possible breaches of the Code of Conduct by agency heads. It was not often that such matters were raised, but they did occur once or twice a year where my personal involvement was necessary. Most of the work was done by commission staff under my direction, ensuring procedural fairness, independent assessment and protection of any whistleblower.

Apart from my statutory responsibilities, I also maintained informal networks among key agency heads, including a monthly lunch of a selected group of the 'old guard' of agency heads. These were not necessarily longstanding secretaries, but a group with very strong personal commitment to the APS and its traditional Westminster values.

There is also a forum of commissioners or equivalent from all Australian jurisdictions. This met at least once a year mostly to share experiences but sometimes to explore opportunities for joint activities. The commissioners sat on an industry training and accreditation board to foster accredited vocational training for public sector employees. They also established a project to develop improved workforce statistics on public sector employees across jurisdictions (the APS Commission's database was the envy of all the other jurisdictions). I also used the network to collect information on processes for appointment, contracts and performance assessment of secretaries and the SES across jurisdictions, which I published in the *State of the Service Report*.

Unlike the Commonwealth–state forums of secretaries, this forum did not work to any ministerial council but set its own agenda.

Internationally, I was involved in three networks:

- the Commonwealth Association of Public Administration and Management (CAPAM), with membership drawn from many Commonwealth countries
- the Pacific Nations' Public Service Commissioners Forum, a less-structured network I encouraged with support from New Zealand
- the Eastern Region Organisation for Public Administration (EROPA), a creature of the United Nations involving practitioners and academics from Asia.

CAPAM was by far the strongest of these. I was on the boards of CAPAM and EROPA, but our finances generally allowed me to travel overseas only once or twice a year. I also had some involvement with the United Nations itself, being invited to speak at a major conference in Mexico and to receive a major award on behalf of the APS in New York.

In 2003, we prepared a book for CAPAM on *Australia's Experience with Public Sector Reform*, drawing together not only Commonwealth initiatives but initiatives across the states. This was a major project in which I took close personal interest, and the book has attracted considerable international interest.

Involvement outside the public sector was limited while I was commissioner. Helen Williams did bequeath me, however, membership of a most useful informal network of top human resources managers, mostly from big private companies. I met the group a couple of times a year over lunch, mostly in Melbourne, where one or two would make a brief presentation on a current issue such as managing cultural change after a company merger, trends in industrial relations or the use of AWAs and workforce planning.

Working with the media

As a statutory officer, I did not feel as inhibited as I did as a secretary in responding to the media. Media interest was, however, generally much more limited, except from a few aficionados. My speeches and commission publications were core aspects of our work and we ensured easy access to them by the APS and the public. On occasions, the media picked them up. I certainly always briefed the media on the *State of the Service Report* (Minister Abbott, however, made it clear he was not too happy about this).

Issues raised: inside or outside the tent?

The issue that was on my mind every day in the commission was the extent to which I was inside the tent, or outside. I was acutely conscious of the danger of being too weak, of not standing up when it counted. If the commissioner does not draw a line in the sand, how can we expect agency heads let alone other APS employees to behave with integrity in upholding the APS Values?

On the other hand, the commissioner is not like the Auditor-General. He or she is not an officer of the Parliament but has a minister with policy authority; the commissioner also has statutory obligations for promoting leadership in the APS and building capability—obligations that necessarily involve being inside the tent—helping agencies to manage their responsibilities and helping the government overall to deliver its policies and programs. These cannot be exercised if the commissioner does not participate in the many forums of secretaries discussing current policy and management challenges.

I suspect I was a little more independent than some other commissioners, but it is interesting that in hindsight my main regrets are that I was not independent enough.

Canberra Times/Public Sector Informant 2002 Christmas edition: Podger admonishing while Moore-Wilton departs, Shergold scooters in and Jane Halton packs away some bandaids in a Christmas stocking. With kind permission from the *Canberra Times* and cartoonist, Pat Campbell.

Table 12.7 My guidelines or the minister's?

The revised *Guidelines on Official Conduct* I issued in 2003 took a long time to finalise. They needed considerable work to line up with the new legislation with its statutory APS Values and Code of Conduct, but I was also keen to canvass a wide range of practical dilemmas public servants faced. Among these was working with ministerial offices with many more advisers than in the past and with wider influence over the Public Service.

While the guidelines would be mine, I felt their influence could be constrained if they did not have broad support among my colleagues or if the minister did not agree with them. Accordingly, I decided to put a draft to the MAC, after first getting some level of comfort from the minister, Tony Abbott.

The minister was not at all impressed with the draft section on working with ministers and their offices. He wanted me to promote a 'seamless' partnership, while I was concerned to clarify the different roles and responsibilities of public servants and advisers and to highlight that advisers had no authority to direct public servants. Over several months, I sent him three different drafts of this section, seeking his reactions and any suggested amendments. At a meeting to discuss the last of these drafts, Abbott told Lynne Tacy and me of his experience as a reporter dealing with a subeditor. 'Sometimes,' he said, 'the subeditor would not try any more to edit an article, but would simply say he doesn't like it. Andrew, I don't like your draft.'

He was challenging me to see if I would stand on my statutory independence. I decided, however, to have one further go at getting his endorsement of our advice, or at least to ask Tacy to do so. Abbott said he would be willing to look at one more draft, but only if it highlighted how a good relationship worked, not what the limits should be.

Tacy did an excellent job, keeping all my concerns in (such as the lack of authority of advisers to direct and the importance of understanding the distinct roles), but only after first describing the ideal form of partnership.

Abbott not only endorsed the next version, he gave the revised guidelines (*my* guidelines as commissioner) public support when they were released. (The guidelines ran into some other interference in the MAC, particularly Max Moore-Wilton's more liberal views than mine on the propriety of accepting hospitality from business, but they clearly benefited from the close scrutiny they received during their development.)

A related issue is the role of the commissioner vis-a-vis that of the Secretary of the Department of PM&C. My view remains that the commissioner should be seen as the professional head of the APS and the Secretary of the Department of PM&C the operational head. In practice, however, that has not been widely endorsed by the people who matter. The commissioner in my time had no statutory role in top appointments, for example. I was also aware that Moore-Wilton was not supportive of the APS Commissioner having equal status with secretaries; Peter Shergold was known to have expressed a similar view from time to time, though on at least one occasion he used my formulation of the commission as a professional head and he as the operational head. My view could hold, however, only if the person appointed commissioner had no lower standing than departmental secretaries, and preferably had significant experience at that level to be able to advise on appointments and on performance with credibility among peers.

I am also of the view that the APS Commission should have responsibility for pay and industrial relations within the APS, not the Department of Employment and Workplace Relations. The latter's focus is inevitably on ensuring the government's wider industrial relations policies are followed in the APS or, better still, modelled in the APS. It is not likely to focus on the business objectives of APS agencies and concern for the capability of the APS as a whole and its upholding of the APS Values. This is a matter of getting the balances right: the APS and APS agencies must operate consistently with the government's wider industrial relations policies, but they should do so with a view to meeting their particular policy and program objectives effectively and efficiently, and to strengthening their capacity to continue to do so into the future.

How prescriptive should the commissioner be in issuing instructions and guidelines? For the most part, the commissioner's directions under the act are not prescriptive, but set out the specific responsibilities of agencies and employees in order to comply with the principles in the act. Beyond that, the commission's approach has been to use guidelines developed cooperatively, rather than rules set from above. Areas where perhaps a firmer stance could be warranted include on classification management and the merit principle and on SES involvement in commission leadership development activities.

The concurrent role of Parliamentary Service Commissioner requires demonstrating independence from the executive arm of government —considerably more so than as Public Service Commissioner. Another challenge is to devote sufficient time and resources to the role. I was assisted by the provision of additional funds for the consultant who helped with the review of the administration of the Parliament, but I had to fund resources for the other work involved from the APS Commission's budget. There would be benefit if the funding for the Parliament included a specific allocation to the commission for the role of Parliamentary Service Commissioner.

Lessons learned as commissioner

Constantly reflecting on whether to be in the tent or outside is healthy. The commissioner might not always come to the right answer, but keeping the balance at the front of one's mind is no bad thing.

Not shirking an issue is an important element of this. If there is an active debate in the APS about any values issue, the commissioner cannot afford to duck it. The commissioner's answer might include a discussion of 'on the one hand' and 'on the other', without an unequivocal judgment in a particular case, but should give genuine guidance on the factors involved and, preferably, a personal weighing up of the arguments, and a view.

The APS Commission's credibility requires it to strengthen its evidence base constantly and to ensure it has top expertise in key areas such as human resource management. The commissioner's own credibility is also vital and relies on past experience and continuing personal learning and development, including through monitoring and discussing developments in and throughout APS agencies.

Clearly, I would like to see some further strengthening of the role of the Public Service Commissioner, who needs to be an experienced CEO with the clout among secretaries to exercise the role. In particular, the commissioner should play a stronger role in succession management.

Table 12.8 Possible further reform agenda for the Australian Public Service Commission

The *Public Service Act 1999* represents the culmination of more than a decade of public sector reform in Australia and remains a good model for a modern public service with a well-embedded culture of professionalism, impartiality and non-partisan responsiveness to elected governments.

There is a need now, however, to reflect on our experience and to make a number of modifications.

1. The commissioner as well as the Secretary of the Department of PM&C should be required to advise (not just provide a report to) the Prime Minister on secretary appointments and on equivalent-level agency head appointments.
2. There should be room to appoint part-time or temporary assistant commissioners along the lines of the Victorian or the Productivity Commission arrangements, to help in agency heads' performance assessments, mentoring and succession management and to undertake specific management reviews from time to time at the request of the minister or the commissioner.
3. The commission should have responsibility for public service pay and conditions and classification management.
4. The coverage of the act should be widened to include most if not all non-commercial and non-military/police agencies.
5. Complementary legislation for the Parliamentary Service and staff of Members of Parliament should be reviewed and updated to include corresponding provisions on values and codes of conduct (reflecting the different roles and responsibilities involved).

> 6. Policies for those employed by Australian Government agencies outside these laws should include the need to specify values and codes of conduct consistent with the public interest.

Endnotes

[1] 'What Really Happens: Departmental Secretary Appointments, Contracts and Performance Pay in the Australian Public Service', *Australian Journal of Public Administration*, June 2007.

13. Some conclusions

The very writing of this monograph has highlighted some of the modern challenges for secretaries and for public administration. How much should a retired secretary reveal about the goings-on in government that were rightly at the time kept confidential? Does revelation by a former secretary, even after two or more elections, make current ministers less trusting of their relationship with current secretaries? Should the rule applying to cabinet papers (foreshadowed recently to be reduced from 30 years to 20 years) be the benchmark, or a shorter period, particularly if no genuinely sensitive information is revealed?

To omit examples of the practices of secretaries and ministers, and the issues involved, would not only make for dull reading, it would remove the real flavour involved. I have tried to steer a middle course, being more open than most of my predecessors have chosen to be in light of the more open society we now live in, which has inter alia already downplayed the old-fashioned public service value of anonymity. I have, however, not written a 'kiss and tell' story or revealed anything particularly sensitive, and nearly all my examples relate to the period before the 2004 election.

Improvements in public administration

During my career in the Public Service, I have seen many changes. Overall, I have no doubt public administration in Australia has improved in these 40 years. The Australian Public Service is more professional and capable than in the past. A simple example illustrates the point: in the 1970s, more than 50 per cent of the APS was at or below what are now the lowest two classification levels (comprising less than 5 per cent of the current APS), most of these not having completed Year 12 schooling, and a small minority of the service were graduates compared with well more than 60 per cent and still rising today. This primarily reflects the impact of new technology, but also the demands of a better-educated and more pluralist society.

In line with the three themes of the Coombs Royal Commission, public administration is also more efficient and effective, more responsive to governments and better engaged with the community it serves.

The financial management reforms of the 1980s and 1990s, led by secretaries such as Ian Castles and Michael Keating, have their detractors, but I have no doubt that these have made the Public Service much more conscious of the taxpayer resources it manages and of the purposes to which Parliament and the public have determined they should be directed. Examples of greater efficiency, and also greater effectiveness, abound, albeit that many reflect successful utilisation of information technology as well as financial management reform. In terms of service delivery, Centrelink today is a vast improvement on the Social Security department I joined in 1978, constantly measuring and reviewing its service performance, utilising the latest technology and linking a wide range of payments on behalf of various Commonwealth and state agencies; the Tax Office's online processes now automatically identify income from many sources, reducing error and speeding up the process; the Job Network is more effective at placing longer-term and disadvantaged unemployed people into jobs than the former Commonwealth Employment Service (CES) and at substantially less cost; even the budget process has been transformed since the 1970s when I was in the Department of the Prime Minister and Cabinet, when the budget had to be 'put to bed' about six weeks before budget night—now decisions can be taken by ministers on the weekend before and be fully incorporated in the documentation tabled on the Tuesday, identifying estimated costs over the forward years along with expected outputs and impacts.

Responsiveness to government has improved through the financial management reforms that have clarified government objectives and improved their capacity to control, and through increased resources for ministers to help them oversee administration, and better cabinet processes. The tiny office Margaret Guilfoyle (Minister for Social Security, 1975–80) occupied in the south-west corner of Old Parliament House in the 1970s had room only for her adviser and a departmental liaison officer, with no meeting space other than her own small room. Today's ministers have large offices, housing several advisers and support staff and a chief of staff and usually two departmental liaison officers, with a separate meeting room and a spacious ministerial room. When working well, the minister's staff and the department operate as a close team complementing their respective roles, ensuring the department is responsive to the minister's requirements in providing professional advice and implementing the government's programs and policies. Cabinet processes are also more elaborate and effective, supported by the Department of the Prime Minister and Cabinet and the other central agencies as well as the Prime Minister's Office and the Cabinet Office.

The administrative law reforms of the late 1970s and early 1980s gave the public and those affected by government administration much greater access and influence, transforming the management of most programs and increasing consistency and effectiveness. The subsequent financial management reforms opened up more opportunities for client influence through service charters and, in some cases, choice of service or service provider through commercialisation, outsourcing and privatisation. More generally, advances in communications, increased media power and more sophisticated approaches by interest groups have contributed to more systematic engagement by agencies with their stakeholders and with the public.

Notwithstanding the continuing political debates involved, I believe there has also been real improvement over the years in public policy in many areas of government activity. To name a few in the social policy field, I would mention superannuation, education and health and aged care. Australia has been fortunate to have successive governments of able and dedicated ministers determined to improve the wellbeing of Australians and willing to pursue longer-term reforms despite short-term political pain. They have been supported by a professional public service led by some remarkable secretaries, notwithstanding some reduction in policy capacity in recent years.

I have had the privilege of participating in many of these developments—in management (the financial management reforms of the 1980s and early 1990s and the people-management reforms of the late 1990s and 2000s) and in policy (poverty alleviation and family allowances in the 1970s, tax and superannuation, youth allowances and higher education in the 1980s, housing and health and aged care in the 1990s and 2000s). Not all have been entirely successful, but my firm judgment is that real progress has been made.

Universal challenges for senior public servants

Many of the challenges facing public administration in Australia are common internationally, because they are driven largely by communications technology and increasing connectedness globally and locally.

Global interdependence, and global 'governance', is affecting the concepts of 'public interest' and 'public goods'. Nations and their governments will still pursue their national interests, but identifying what is truly in the national interest requires understanding of global public interests and how they might best be protected and promoted. Harmonisation of government regulation and policy is increasingly important, whether in social policy fields such as public health (including food safety and therapeutic goods and managing the risks of communicable diseases) or in financial markets, and the pressure for world authorities to ensure justice and human rights or to regulate international trade and business is also increasing.

Nearly every national agency these days has a substantial and growing international agenda, requiring the development and maintenance of international networks of officials to support international forums of ministers and guide the work of international organisations. Politicians also need to develop their own international networks.

Departmental secretaries (and their equivalents in other nations) have particular responsibilities in ensuring the development and nurturing of these networks and must be personally involved. They must contribute to the international forums and help their governments respond to emerging policies. This requires investment, particularly in staff moving into more senior positions and those with the potential to be secretaries in the future. I experienced a huge shift over my career from the days when every overseas visit needed the approval of the Overseas Visits Committee to when most senior executives would travel overseas at least once every two years. From my first visit to the OECD in 1980, I found enormous value in having an international perspective on the policies I was developing and reviewing. My contributions to international policy development were modest, but that role will be increasingly important for secretaries and other senior officials in the years to come and will involve increased mobility between the Australian public service and international organisations.

Improved communications and a better-educated and wealthier community have also, as mentioned, led to more systematic engagement by Australian government agencies with their domestic stakeholders and the Australian public. This will only continue to grow, with secretaries needing to employ increasingly sophisticated approaches to communications management. Secretaries' ability to manage by Weberian processes of hierarchical control will also continue to diminish, as staff and those outside their departments expect to be consulted and to have real influence, and secretaries' own influence over ministers is challenged by the contributions of others. Concepts such as 'governance' and 'leadership', which encompass a more diffused process of decision making, are likely to grow in importance and in complexity as governments strive to respond to rapid change and uncertainty. In this environment, values including integrity and impartiality are fundamental to fostering productive relationships.

The perennial issue of the political–administrative interface, and of the balance between the responsiveness and independence of the Public Service, has been affected everywhere by the communications revolution. Australia's moves since the 1980s to increase responsiveness have been mirrored in nearly all Western democracies, with closer control by political leaders, more political staff and more carefully managed media relations. As I have argued elsewhere,[1] there is reason for concern that the legitimate push for increased responsiveness in Australia has now gone too far, unduly constraining public service independence. Recent actions by the Rudd Government on secretaries' contracts and performance pay, ministerial staff numbers and conduct, and senior appointments have gone some way to redress the balance, but the problem is even more acute among state governments, and the underlying pressures remain, requiring constant care and attention. It is more common these days for secretaries to be called on to defend ministers than, as was accepted practice formerly, for ministers to defend officials.

There is no simple answer here. A key element of public service professionalism is the democratic responsibility to be responsive; some independence is also demanded by the values of impartiality and being non-partisan. I always highlighted the caveat to the view commonly expressed in the 1980s and 1990s that public servants did not determine the public interest because that was for the elected government to decide. The caveat is 'subject to the law', and I would highlight the role of public servants in upholding this through due process as determined by public service, financial management and administrative law, and through common law interpretations of that legislation. These laws include very broad concepts such as values (*Public Service Act*), ethics (*Financial Management and Accountability Act*) and public interest (for example, *Freedom of Information Act*), which govern due process. If anything, I would take this further, suggesting public servants are also responsible for advising on good processes for policy development as well as program administration, beyond the strict requirements of the law. In my view, the Public Service does, in this wide area of due process, truly have responsibility to identify and protect the public interest.

More recently, the idea of 'public value' has gained currency, encouraging public servants to be more than just responsive and to exercise leadership to ensure policies and programs add public value in addressing community problems. I have much sympathy for this but am also mindful that our Westminster system does require ministers to accept responsibility and be accountable to Parliament; taking too far public servants' responsibility to deliver 'public value' could undermine this principle. Secretaries need to guard against their officers being too independently minded and critical of the political process, as well as against excessive responsiveness, which can undermine due process.

Particular Australian challenges

Australia's federal system imposes particular constraints on the national government and affects most secretaries considerably. Few informed people argue for abolition of the states, recognising not only history but the extent to which federalist factors are built into nearly every aspect of the constitution, including the structure of the legislature, the role and structure of the judiciary, as well as the responsibilities that can be exercised by the Executive (and the Parliament). Most also recognise that there are efficiencies in a degree of devolution and decentralisation, along with greater capacity to respond to the varying needs of different communities.

Nonetheless, federal arrangements are under increasing pressure, driven again by communications and transport technology and associated global forces. Increased international activity inevitably adds to the role of national governments and changes in the way business is managed within Australia and the way people move and communicate also add to demand for national consistency and coherence. There is also evidence of an increased national identity among Australians.

National approaches do not, however, necessarily require exclusive national government authority: state governments might agree to harmonise their policies or they might contribute to national policies adding their practical experience to the deliberative process or they might administer agreed nationally consistent approaches.

Nonetheless, the purview of the national government is inexorably widening in my view and reliance on cooperation and goodwill without some fundamental reconsideration of roles and responsibilities will prove eventually to be too slow and bureaucratic, and ineffective. Secretaries of Australian government departments do need to have increased appreciation of the policy and management issues faced by their state counterparts, whether or not formal changes in roles and responsibilities are on the agenda.

Another particular issue for Australia concerns the balance of power between the Executive, the legislature and the judiciary. The role of the judiciary and quasi-judicial institutions widened substantially with the administrative law reforms 30 years ago, largely in response to the increasing, and increasingly complex, role of government administration. Notwithstanding the role of Senate Committees, it is the legislature that is struggling to keep pace with the continuing increase in government activity.

Along with most secretaries, I was frustrated by the style of most of the Senate Committees I attended, which rarely addressed the major policy or performance issues and mostly pursued more superficial and immediate political matters. I believe these committees need more professional support from the Parliamentary Service, rather than from political staff, to probe more deeply and over time substantial policy and performance matters. House of Representatives Committees have even further to go to provide the level of scrutiny needed. The media might be largely to blame, but it too responds to the material provided, including by Parliament and its committees and individual politicians.

Secretaries might not welcome more scrutiny, but they would welcome a shift in the scrutiny towards issues of substance. This might also enhance the understanding by Members of Parliament, including potential future ministers, of the operation of the Public Service and the capacity of its senior leaders (other than their political dexterity).

Final comments

I have had the privilege of being a public servant for 37 years, including 12 years as a secretary or equivalent. It was a period of great change in the Public Service and in government, through the excitement of the Whitlam years, the steadier hand of the Fraser era, the years of economic and financial management reform under Hawke and Keating and the conservative pragmatism of the Howard Government. All were reformist governments in their own way. Each ended up, even if not by prior intention, presiding over an extension of the role of the Australian Government both domestically and internationally. The means of achieving that role shifted, particularly under the Hawke, Keating and Howard Governments, towards purchasing and regulating rather than providing. Governments and the Public Service also responded to increasing community expectations and advances in technology, with increasing concern for service delivery and policy implementation as well as policy development and advising, and with increasing demand for community engagement and responsiveness to individual circumstances and preferences.

This monograph focuses on the changing role of departmental secretaries, but the context is of the changing role of government and changing approaches to public administration. I have included in Appendix B a summary of the main reforms to which I contributed; Appendix C includes a list of some of my publications and those official publications to which I made a substantial contribution.

No doubt changes will continue, particularly as technological development continues to accelerate. The unique role of the Public Service, however, and of its leadership is likely to continue based, in my view, on the core values of professionalism, impartiality, responsiveness, non-partisanship, accountability and service.

Endnotes

Podger, A. 2007a, 'What really happens: departmental secretary appointments, contracts and performance pay in the Australian Public Service', *Australian Journal of Public Administration*, vol. 66, no. 2, June, pp. 131–47.

Appendix A

Public service career

Years	Agency	Position	Ministers
1968–73	Australian Bureau of Statistics	Cadet, Research Officer	
1974–75	Social Welfare Commission	Senior Research Officer (now EL1)	Bill Hayden, John Wheeldon
1975–78	Prime Minister and Cabinet	Class 10/11 (EL2)	Gough Whitlam, Malcolm Fraser
1978–82	Social Security	Branch Head (SES1)	Margaret Guilfoyle, Fred Chaney
1982–90	Finance	Branch Head (SES1) Division Head (SES2)	Margaret Guilfoyle, John Dawkins, Peter Walsh, Ralph Willis
1990–93	Defence	Deputy Secretary (SES3)	Robert Ray, John Faulkner, Roger Price, Gary Punch
1993–94	Administrative Services and the Arts	Secretary	Bob McMullan, Frank Walker
1994–96	Housing and Regional Development	Secretary	Brian Howe, Mary Crawford
1996–2002	Health and Family Services; Health and Aged Care	Secretary	Michael Wooldridge, Judi Moylan, Bob Woods, Trish Worth, Warwick Smith, Bronwyn Bishop, Grant Tambling, Kay Patterson, Kevin Andrews
2002–04	Australian Public Service Commission	Public Service Commissioner	John Howard, Tony Abbott, Kevin Andrews
2004–05	Prime Minister and Cabinet	Chair, Review of Health Services Delivery	John Howard

Appendix B

Career highlights

Dates	Activity
1971	Papua New Guinea Census
1972–73	Henderson Poverty Inquiry
1974–75	Childcare Review
	Income security strategies and directions (including on poverty alleviation, national superannuation and national compensation)
1975–76	Income Security Review — Family Allowance reform
1977	Personal income tax reform
1978–82	Work on social security and tax, defence of universal family allowances, tax expenditure
1983	Reform of housing assistance
	Reform of superannuation and age pension arrangements
1985	Involvement in tax reform
1986	New compensation scheme for the Public Service
1987	Reform of youth allowances (student assistance, unemployment benefits)
	Abolition of the Public Service Board and restructuring of portfolio departments
1988	Museums review
	Involvement in introduction of Higher Education Contribution Scheme (HECS)
1990	Involvement in review of military superannuation
1991–93	Defence Commercial Support Program
	Over-the-horizon radar project
	Sale of ASTA and ADI
	Defence industry policy
1994	Regional Economic Development program and extension of Better Cities
1995	Proposals for public housing reform (agreed by COAG but never implemented)
1996	Aged-care reforms
	General practice enhancement
	Coordinated care trials
1997	Separation of Medibank Private from Health Insurance Commission
	Strengthening cost-effectiveness basis for PBS
	Rural health initiatives
	Establishing Health Services Australia
1998	Negotiating Australian Health Care Agreements
1999	Private health insurance lifetime cover reform
	Doubling NHMRC budget
2003	New Guidelines on Official Conduct and Embedding APS Values
	Enhanced *State of the Service Report*
2004	Integrated Leadership System for the APS
2005	Review for Prime Minister of health services delivery

Appendix C

Key publications by Andrew Podger

'Expenditures on social welfare in Australia, 1900–70', in R. Mendelsohn 1979, *The Condition of the People*, Allen & Unwin.

The relationship between the social security and personal income tax systems: a practical examination, Development Division Research Paper No. 9, 1980 [with Raymond and Jackson]. Also published in R. Mendelsohn (ed.) 1983, *Social Welfare Finance: Selected papers*.

Taxation expenditures—submission by the Department of Social Security to the Inquiry into Taxation Expenditures by the House of Representatives Standing Committee on Expenditure, Development Division Research Paper No. 17, 1982 [with Ingles, Raymond and Jackson].

What price heritage? The Museums Review and the measurement of museum performance, Department of Finance Discussion Paper, 1989 [with Ross Martin].

'Retirement incomes policy: options open to the government', ANU Seminar Series on Finance of Old Age, November 1984, in R. Mendelsohn 1986, *Finance of Old Age*, Allen & Unwin.

'Economics of superannuation', *The Australian Economic Review*, 3 October 1986, pp. 77–86.

Defence industry policy, Government Policy Paper, AGPS, 1990.

Community and nation, Government Policy Paper on Housing and Regional Development Reform, AGPS, 1995 [key contributor].

'Lessons for housing and regional development', in Uhr and Mackay (eds) 1996, *Evaluating Policy Advice: Learning from Commonwealth experience*, The Australian National University.

'Departmental secretaries: introductory notes', *Australian Journal of Public Administration*, vol. 56, no. 4, December 1997, pp. 11–12.

'Reforming the Australian health care system: a government perspective', *Health Affairs*, May–June 1999.

'Reforming the Australian health care system: the role of government', [with Hagan] in Abby Bloom (ed.) 1999, *Health Reform in Australia and New Zealand*, Oxford University Press.

'Policy learning and health', *Australian Journal of Public Administration*, March 2000.

'Australia's balance between public and private arrangements', *Health Affairs*, May–June 2000.

'Communicating with the public', *The Public Interest*, December 2001–January 2002.

'Defining an Australian approach to the roles and values of the Public Service in the 21st century', *Canberra Bulletin of Public Administration*, vol. 104, June 2002, pp. 1–5.

APS Values and Code of Conduct in Practice, Australian Public Service Commission, August 2003 [main author, issued under my authority].

Embedding APS Values, Australian Public Service Commission, August 2003 [issued under my authority].

Australia's Experience with Public Sector Reform, Australian Public Service Commission 2003; also published by CAPAM [key contributor, issued under my authority].

Report of the Review of the Administration of the Parliament, Canberra, 2003 [as Parliamentary Service Commissioner].

'Innovation with integrity—the public sector leadership imperative to 2020', *Australian Journal of Public Administration*, March 2004.

Managing the interface with ministers and the Parliament, Senior Executive Service breakfast presentation, 23 April 2004, <www.apsc.gov.au>

'Hutton Inquiry: some Australian reaction', *Canberra Bulletin of Public Administration*, March 2004.

Integrated Leadership System, Australian Public Service Commission, June 2004 [issued under my authority].

Some parting remarks on the Australian Public Service, Retirement speech, 30 June 2005, published in *The Canberra Times' Public Sector Informant*, 5 July 2005.

'Directions for health reform in Australia', *Productive Federalism, Proceedings of a Roundtable*, Productivity Commission, February 2006.

A model health system for Australia, Inaugural Menzies Centre Lecture on Public Health Policy, Menzies Centre for Public Health Policy, 3 February 2006, published as a series of articles in the *Asia Pacific Journal of Health Management* in 2006 (vol. 1, nos 1, 2) and 2007 (vol. 2, no. 1).

Report of the Inquiry into the Culture of ADF Schools and Training Establishments, Department of Defence, December 2006 [other committee members were Catherine Harris and Major-General Roger Powell].

'What really happens: departmental secretary appointments, contracts and performance pay in the Australian Public Service', *Australian Journal of Public Administration*, vol. 66, no. 2, June 2007, pp. 131–47.

Report of the Review of Military Superannuation, Department of Defence, December 2007 [other committee members were David Knox and Air Commodore Lee Roberts].

Appendix D

References

Australian Public Service Commission 2003a, *APS Values and Code of Conduct in Practice* [otherwise known as *Guidelines on Official Conduct*].

Australian Public Service Commission 2003b, *Australia's Experience with Public Sector Reform*.

Australian Public Service Commission 2003c, *Embedding the Values*.

Australian Public Service Commission 2004, *Integrated Leadership System*.

Australian Public Service Commission 2008, *Merit-Based Appointments*.

Ayers, A. J. 1996, 'Not like the good old days: Garran Oration', *Australian Journal of Public Administration*, vol. 55, no. 2, June, pp. 3–12.

Beddie, Francesca 2001, *'Putting Life Into Years'—The Commonwealth's role in Australia's health since 1901*, Department of Health and Aged Care.

Bridgeman, P. and Davis, G. 1998, *Australian Policy Handbook*, Second edition, Allen & Unwin.

Castles, I. 1984, *Economists and anti-economists. Presidential address to the fifty-fourth ANZAAS Congress*, ANZAAS monograph.

Castles, I. 1987, 'Facts and fantasies of bureaucracy', *Canberra Bulletin of Public Administration*, December, pp. 35–45.

Clarke, I. and Swain, H. 2007, 'Distinguishing the real from the surreal in management reform', *Canadian Public Administration*, vol. 48, no. 4, pp. 453–76.

Codd, M. 1990, *The role of secretaries of departments in the APS*, Senior Executive Staffing Unit Occasional Paper No. 8, Public Service Commission.

Cooley, A. S. 1974, 'The permanent head', *Public Administration (Sydney)*, vol. XXXIII, no. 3, September, pp. 193–205.

Crawford, J. 1954, 'The role of the permanent head', *Public Administration (Sydney)*, September.

Crawford, J. 1970, 'Relations between civil servants and ministers in policy making', *Australian Journal of Public Administration*, vol. 19, no. 2, pp. 99–112.

Hyslop, R. 1993, *Australian Mandarins: Perceptions of the role of departmental secretaries*, AGPS Press in association with the Public Service Commission and the Royal Institute of Public Administration Australia, Canberra.

Hyslop, R. 1998, *A Very Civil Servant: An Australian memoire*, Clarion Editions, Binalong, New South Wales.

Management Advisory Committee 2001, *Performance Management in the APS: A strategic framework*, Australian Public Service Commission.

Management Advisory Committee 2004, *Connected Government*, Australian Public Service Commission.

Northcote, S. H. and Trevelyan, C. E. 1853, *Report on the Organisation of the Permanent Civil Service*, United Kingdom.

Podger, A. 2007a, 'What really happens: departmental secretary appointments, contracts and performance pay in the Australian Public Service', *Australian Journal of Public Administration*, vol. 66, no. 2, June, pp. 131–47.

Podger, A. 2007b, 'Response to Peter Shergold', *Australian Journal of Public Administration*, vol. 66, no. 4, December, pp. 498–500.

Senge, P. 1990, *The Fifth Discipline*, Currency Doubleday.

Shergold, P. 2007, 'What really happens in the Australian Public Service: an alternative view', *Australian Journal of Public Administration*, vol. 66, no. 3, September, pp. 367–70.

Spann, R. N. 1976, 'Permanent heads', *Report of the Royal Commission on Australian Government Administration*, AGPS, Appendix 1.I.

Uhrig, J. 2004, *Report of the Review of the Governance of Statutory Authorities and Statutory Officeholders*, Department of Finance and Administration.

Walsh, P. 1996, *Confessions of a Failed Finance Minister*, Random House Australia.

Weller, P. 2001, *Australia's Mandarins: The frank and the fearless?*, Allen & Unwin.

Weller, P. and Wanna, J. 1997, 'Departmental secretaries: appointment, termination and their impact', *Australian Journal of Public Administration*, vol. 56, no. 4, December, pp. 13–25.

www.ingramcontent.com/pod-product-compliance
Lightning Source LLC
Chambersburg PA
CBHW061239270326

41926CB00075B/4675